NON-TRADITIONAL ENTRANTS
TO HIGHER EDUCATION
'They talk about people like me'

NON-TRADITIONAL ENTRANTS TO HIGHER EDUCATION
'They talk about people like me'

Marion Bowl

Trentham Books
Stoke on Trent, UK and Sterling USA

Trentham Books Limited

Westview House	22883 Quicksilver Drive
734 London Road	Sterling
Oakhill	VA 20166-2012
Stoke on Trent	USA
Staffordshire	
England ST4 5NP	

2003 © Marion Bowl

First published 2003

British Library Cataloguing-in-Publication Data
A catalogue record for this book is available from the British Library

ISBN 1 85856 298 8

Designed and typeset by Trentham Print Design Ltd., Chester and printed in Great Britain by Cromwell Press Ltd., Wiltshire.

CONTENTS

PART TWO
PARADOXES IN WIDENING PARTICIPATION

*They talk about people like me in Social Policy –
with disadvantage. I feel as if I'm living social
policy rather than just reading it from textbooks,
which other students are.*

Salma

ACKNOWLEDGEMENTS

The research process, which has resulted in the production of this book has required the active participation of people who would normally remain anonymous. However, a group of women who agreed to speak up publicly about their experiences of higher education deserve to be thanked by name. To Shahnaz Bibi, Marcia Boothe, Carol D'Caccio, Jacqui Edwards, Andrea Housen, Gwen Lovell, Norma Hofmann, Carol Robinson and Taleebah Selassie go my heartfelt thanks for their time, commitment and courage, as well as their personal support. To other research participants who have not been named go my thanks for their contribution to the research and their patience in answering my questions, listening to my ideas and inspiring the book.

Thanks also to friends and colleagues who have taken time to read and comment on my work: Leone Burton, Ann Davis, Tim Davies, Lynn Goode Wendy Fox-Kirk, Barbara Hepburn, Chris Hockings, Joan O'Hagan, Kate O'Malley, Gail Walters and Lis Whitelaw.

The opportunity to undertake the research on which this book is based came as a result of my employment with Birmingham Reachout and therefore I am grateful to the staff of Newtown/Ladywood Task Force, which was responsible for funding Reachout from 1996 to 1998 and to members of the Reachout Steering Group who helped to guide its work over that period.

INTRODUCTION

I hear that there is going to be a better chance for such helpless students as I was. There are schemes afoot for making the University less exclusive and extending its influence.

Thomas Hardy: *Jude the Obscure*, 1895.
Re-published 1969, p. 413

Who is this book for?

This book is for anyone who has an interest in social justice in education. It is dedicated to those who have struggled against barriers of lack of information, support and finance and who have made their way to higher education, against the odds. The book is addressed to careers advisors, teachers, tutors and academics who are responsible on a day-to-day basis for ensuring that equity in education is made a reality. It is also addressed to those working to widen participation in higher education, from within the university or outside it. Finally, this book is addressed to those in government and in higher education institutions who are responsible for planning, financing and directing educational resources.

The book explores to what extent widening participation is a reality in the twenty-first century and whether the increase in numbers of students in higher education really means the dawning of an age of equality of opportunity, experience and rewards. It offers the findings and recommendations from the practice of one widening participation and action research project, but hopefully its recommendations will have wider

1

value. Hopefully too, it will encourage an examination of the way in which the practices of education, and particularly higher education, may be at odds with the policy of widening participation. My aim in writing this book is also to make a contribution towards changing some of those conscious and unconscious practices which continue to exclude mature, working class and ethnic minority students from enjoying the benefits of university study.

The context

Concern with widening access to higher education in the United Kingdom is not new. At the turn of the nineteenth century, it was enough of an issue for Thomas Hardy to depict Jude at the gates of Oxford University, beguiled by its ethos, but unable to enter. One hundred years later, the persistence of class, gender and race inequalities in access to higher education is an enduring feature of discussions among academics and policy makers.

Since its election in 1997, the Labour Government has stressed the importance of widening the social class base of the university student population. In its consultative document, *The Learning Age* (DfEE 1998a) the new government committed itself to increasing and widening participation in higher education. It pledged itself to creating more university places and anticipated that mature students would take up half these additional places. It also made additional funding available to support universities in their efforts to widen participation.

Since 1999, the number of government initiatives to widen participation has continued to grow. A new proposal for extending participation *Partnerships for Progression* (HEFCE 2001) has been launched. The government has set a target of 50 per cent participation in higher education of those aged eighteen to thirty by the year 2010. In the past five years, policy pronouncements have come thick and fast on the issue of lifelong learning, equity of access to higher education and the participation in higher education of those designated non-traditional students by virtue of their income, class, age or ethnicity.

At the same time, there has been an increased research interest in widening participation in higher education. This has resulted in a growing literature on the subject of access to higher education (Merrill 1999,

Preece 1999, Plummer 2000, Burke 2002). This book makes a contribution to that discussion. It explores the reality of access to higher education from the perspectives of a group of people from working class and ethnic minority backgrounds. The research on which this book is based addresses issues not dealt with in any depth in policy reports on widening access: the impact of the policy agenda on the lives of those who have traditionally been excluded from higher educational opportunities. It views the impact of this agenda from a perspective which is often overlooked: the perspective of the student rather than of the policy maker or the educational institution.

The research for this book took place between 1997 and 2001, a period during which government policy changes in the area of widening access to higher education were beginning to be implemented. It therefore provides an opportunity to compare policy statements and initiatives aimed at widening participation with the day to day experiences of non-traditional students themselves. It explores the early aspirations and educational experiences of a group of people who opted to take advantage of a new climate in educational thinking. It also explores the everyday reality of access, widening participation and lifelong learning for those who enter university as mature students with family, work and caring commitments. It draws on the contributions of thirty-two people who became involved with the Birmingham Reachout Project, a central government, community based initiative aimed at increasing mature, working class and ethnic minority entry to higher education.

I am grateful to the students who have been willing to give up their time to relate their experiences to me, to offer their advice to others thinking of going down a similar path and to speak in a more public forum about their experiences as newcomers to and, to some extent, outsiders in higher education.

1

ABOUT THE RESEARCH

The Reachout Project: a research opportunity

The Birmingham Reachout project was the outcome of a loose partnership between a group of education professionals. They collaborated to gain funding to set up a project aimed at adults who wished to return to education but who were unable to attend college based Access Courses because of family or work commitments or disability. Reachout was initially funded by a central government initiative which sought to improve the employment prospects of people living in an area of Birmingham labelled disadvantaged by virtue of its poor employment opportunities and high levels of socio-economic deprivation. The project was implicitly aimed at women. It was also implicitly aimed at working class women who were of African-Caribbean or South Asian origin. It has become customary in the educational world to refer to adult students from disadvantaged backgrounds as non-traditional students.

I was appointed in 1996 as the project's co-ordinator and its only full-time worker. Funding was also made available to employ a part-time administrative assistant and a small team of hourly paid tutors whose role was to teach and provide support for participants wishing to progress to higher education. Freed of some of the constraints of further education college funding, Reachout was able to develop its work in response to its students' expressed needs, and to take a highly student centred approach. It provided:

- Impartial and sustained advice, guidance and support to adults wishing to progress educationally

- A Social Science based access to a higher education course aimed specifically at adults with childcare or work commitments. Course participants could follow their studies on a flexible basis, either in a local group, on a drop-in basis or from home, with tutor support. They could study at a pace which suited them – over one year or less, two years or more.

- Residential weekends and day courses designed to prepare participants for university. These courses included study skills preparation, help with applying to university, financial advice and familiarisation visits to the local university.

- Help with childcare and travel costs to enable study, as well as assistance with finding cheap or second hand computers and books.

As well as offering opportunities for local people to consider moving on educationally, the Reachout project offered a unique opportunity to research in some depth the challenges and obstacles facing non-traditional students who wish to study at undergraduate level. It afforded the possibility of developing a participatory approach (Carr and Kemmis 1986) to exploring students' perspectives on access to higher education. The participants described in this book were almost all non-traditional university entrants in terms of their age, educational background, ethnicity, gender and social class position. It could be argued that all are benefiting from political and policy changes in post-sixteen education during the late 1990s.

This book addresses the issue of non-traditional students' access to higher education from a standpoint rarely addressed: looking at the university from outside rather than from within, attempting to capture students' perspectives in depth through a longitudinal approach and through adopting a methodology which placed their voices and their views of what it is to be a non-traditional student in the foreground. From my position as both researcher and community based education worker, I have tried to make recommendations for practical action, both in the way community based widening participation initiatives like Reachout operate and in the way educational institutions and workers view non-traditional students and their learning.

Approaching the research

My starting point for the research was practical, and I began with the essentially practical questions which had occurred to me as I went about my work:

Why?
- did certain adults decide to return to study after a break of three or more years?
- did they not continue to higher education earlier in their lives?

What?
- were adults' experiences of returning to study, at access and higher education levels?
- factors inhibited or encouraged their progress on returning to study?
- were the perceived advantages and disadvantages of returning to study?

How?
- could the progress of adult students be optimised?
- could equality of educational and career opportunity be assured for women, black and working class students?

Through discussion with participants, I wished to gain some understanding of their perspectives and the ways in which the Reachout project might help them achieve their educational aims. Through inviting their participation in disseminating and discussing the research conclusions, I have tried to create a situation where we could jointly voice our views on areas where change was seen to be desirable. This approach has enabled me to invite those who were directly affected by the work of the project to contribute to its development and the evaluation of its effectiveness. I have sought to engage in participatory action research (Kemmis and Wilkinson 1998), to involve participants in the process of the research, to gain a deeper understanding of the issues that affect them and with them to begin to find ways in which we can work for change.

The participants in this study were principally, but not entirely, women bringing up children single-handed. It appeared to me that they had been denied the opportunity to achieve their educational aspirations earlier in life. This book therefore tells a story which is mainly but not exclusively about women. The Reachout project tended to attract women aged twenty-five to forty-five who had children of school age. In deciding to return to study, they were, unwittingly or otherwise, entering a world where knowledge, 'truth' and success are still largely defined by white males (Davies *et al* 1994). Although in recent years, concern has been expressed at men's absence from return to study and access courses (McGivney 1999), and their seeming disaffection with education, perhaps the question which has not been addressed is why women, against all the odds, and faced with the immense barriers of lack of finance and lack of adequate childcare and support, are opting to work towards university entry.

There is evidence (for example, Edwards 1993, Lunneborg 1994, Parr 2000, Plummer 2000) that women entering higher education later in life have tended to be directed into stereotypic career paths. They experience particular conflicts and barriers which relate to their gender positions as mothers, frequently as lone carers, and as workers directed towards particular occupational roles with poor wage and career structures. Feminist research (Oakley 1981, Lather 1991) aims to introduce women's perspectives into issues of public concern, but, above all, to produce knowledge which can be used by women to create change.

The particular questions which I wished my research to address for women were:

Why do they decide to return to education and aim for higher education?

How do they experience returning to education and entry to higher education?

What barriers, costs and opportunities does higher education bring with it?

The research also became a story mainly but not entirely about black women: black British, black Caribbean, black African, British Asian, Indian, Pakistani and Bangladeshi women. There was considerable diversity in their experience of education in this country and elsewhere. Ostensibly, what they shared was their decision to consider returning to study as mature students, and to aim for higher education entry after a break from school education of more than three years.

As a white, single, child free woman who has, through education, assumed some of the norms and values of a middle class woman (Mahony 1997, Lynch 1999), I have had cause to reflect on the basis on which I could conduct research of this kind. I am aware that, in interviewing black women and men during the course of this research, I was hearing a story told to a white researcher. I have no doubt that the nature of disclosures made to me would have been quite different had I been a black female interviewing black students, and different again had I been a black male researcher interviewing black women students. The stories we tell and are told will vary according to assumptions made about the listener and her understanding of, for example, racism. I can only understand racism from a white perspective, not from the perspective of someone who has experienced it from day to day (Burton 1993).

Is it legitimate for a white researcher to conduct research with black people? On the other hand, is it legitimate to carry out research which excludes black people? For me, the latter position is unjustifiable. Patricia Hill Collins (1991) criticises white female researchers who seek to dodge the issue of including black women:

> ... white women who possess great competence in researching a range of issues omit women of color from their work, claiming that they are unqualified to understand the 'Black woman's experience' ... reflect a basic unwillingness by many white feminists to alter the paradigms that guide their work. (p. 10)

However, there are dangers for a white researcher to purport to be doing empowering research with black participants. In the idea of empowerment, there is more than a suspicion of colonialism. There is also a danger in researching black experiences that the black person becomes the problem to be researched, instead of the institutions and structures within which racism is perpetuated (Bhavnani 1988, 1994). In researching within an antiracist framework, I have striven to ensure that I do not constitute being black (or female, or working class) as the problem. Rather, I have tried to enable the voices of people involved in education to be heard directly and to ensure that I do not stand between the researched and the audience for research.

I cannot speak from the multiple perspectives of those with whom I have spent so many hours talking, questioning and working. I can only construct a story from a standpoint, which strives to be antisexist, antiracist and anticlassist (hooks 1984, Harding 1987, Collins 1991, Mahony (ed.) 1997, Lynch 1999) and which can stand up to the scrutiny of those who have been involved in the research.

I have tried to conduct and use the research data in ways which enable myself and others to see a reality more clearly, as a precursor to trying to change it. I hope that this is apparent in the chapters which follow.

The research process

An important aspect of the research process was its attempt to encourage participants to use their own voices to express the nature of the problems they experienced in gaining access to and operating within higher education.

One of the implications of such an approach was that it depended on closeness and trust between myself as researcher and those who in other research designs might be referred to as *the research subjects* or *respondents*. In this way, I also hoped to gain a richer picture (Simons 1980, Stake 1995) of the place of education in the lives of those with whom I worked. Such an approach had the advantage of making it possible to bring to the surface issues not immediately obvious to myself as a teacher and researcher – someone whose educational background did not involve juggling the complex demands of family, finance, care and relationships. It also made it possible to look at changes in students' perspectives over time and at the effects of a move into higher education on the daily lives of adults.

In the course of my daily work and in the first year of the project, my main source of data collection was informal discussion and personal reflection on issues emerging as important in impeding or assisting participants' progress towards their education goals. It was an open-ended way of exploring participants' perceptions of what issues were relevant to them. I did not carry out more formal interviews until we had come to know one another quite well. The aim of the first seventeen individual interviews, which took place towards the end of the first year of the project, was to begin to build a picture of the lives and educational histories of the Reachout participants who had been involved with the Reachout project thus far. The stories of these participants are told in chapters two and three.

A further round of interviews was carried out between November 1997 and September 1998 with another thirteen participants, whom I had known for a year or more and who had developed a clear idea that they wished to move towards higher education. These interviews provided a more formal and focused way of raising questions. Of the thirteen people interviewed, nine had already moved on to full or part-time higher education. The remaining four participants had expressed the intention to apply for university entry or professional training within the coming months. The focus for the second round of interviews was to continue to build a picture of participants' educational backgrounds and to listen to their stories of their progress, both positive and negative. It was from this group of thirteen students, as well as those in the first group who had moved on to higher education, that I sought further involvement in the later phases of the project.

Collectivising experience: the *Students Speak* conference

The next phase of the research, which lasted from September 1998 to March 1999, was an attempt to begin to define collectively the concerns which participants had already voiced. It entailed asking participants to express directly to an interested audience some of the concerns they had expressed to one another and to me during the first two years of Reachout's existence. I sought their involvement in planning and con-tributing to a conference entitled *Students Speak*, aimed at promoting discussion between non-traditional students, tutors and policy makers. I presented a number of options for involvement, including public speak-ing at the conference, co-facilitating conference workshops and com-menting on and suggesting amendments to a conference report, based on the first two years of the research.

Nine women agreed to act as conference speakers. Four group sessions were organised before the conference to help participants write and deliver their contributions to the conference and develop their public speaking skills. Those who helped to organise the conference gave their time and effort freely and generously. The joint activity around organis-ing and speaking at the conference brought the ten of us together in a relationship which has continued over more than four years.

The *Students Speak* conference took place in December 1998. It attracted over eighty students, academics and policy makers. The first part of the conference was based on a report of the first stage of the research (Bowl 1998) and the verbal contributions of nine mature women students from non-traditional backgrounds and myself. We acted as keynote speakers, each making a brief contribution on the problems faced by non-traditional students entering higher institutions.

Eight of the student participants were of African-Caribbean origin and one was of Pakistani origin. Seven of the nine women had small children; all but one had started a university course in the preceding twelve months; four were studying part-time and five full-time.

The second part of the conference involved workshop sessions. These were facilitated jointly by Reachout tutors and students. Each workshop focused on one of the themes which had emerged as important in hindering non-traditional students' progress towards or within higher education. The aims for the workshops were to encourage discussion between students and academics and to bring forward recommendations and suggested solutions to some of the issues raised at the conference. The conference enabled people located in different positions of power within higher education to come together and discuss issues of mutual interest. It gave time and space specifically for students themselves to express their concerns, and it facilitated the production of specific and realistic recommendations for future action. These recommendations have been incorporated into the final part of this book.

The final phase of data collection involved in-depth, tape-recorded interviews with ten of the participants at the end of their first year of study. They were encouraged to look back on the year and to explore their developing relationships with the institutions they entered, their course work, their tutors and peers. They reflected on what they had said two years before and whether their perceptions had changed. Five of those I interviewed at this stage had also been involved as speakers in the *Students Speak* conference.

Finally, I carried out a follow-up interview with Salma, one of the first former Reachout students to graduate from university. She had been involved with the Reachout project, the *Students Speak* conference and the research from its earliest stage. She was therefore able to provide me with insights on her own development, as well as on the impact of our endeavours over almost four years. For this reason, an edited transcript of our final conversation, which took place shortly after she received her degree result, forms the concluding chapter of this book.

A note on style and structure
Part One of this book (chapters two to seven) tells some of the stories of the research participants in two ways: first, by relating individuals' own

descriptions of their experiences, which expressed particularly vividly some of the themes arising from the interviews and discussions; second, by linking some of the themes which emerged during my analysis to the relevant literature. In Part Two, chapters eight and nine link the research findings to more theoretical, overarching explanations about the links between social and economic disadvantage and systems of education (Bourdieu 1966, 1977, 1979, 1997, Bourdieu and Passeron 1977, Apple 1990,1991,1993). Chapters ten and eleven discuss the implications for practice, policy and future research.

A note on presentation

In Part One the descriptive sections of each chapter are presented through the stories of participants. I have tried to intrude as little as possible upon what participants had to say but I have made some editorial decisions. For the sake of clarity, I have sometimes reordered a section of an interview, to emphasise a particular point or to put it in a more logical and meaningful place. I have also removed the hesitations and any mistaken pronunciations which appeared in transcripts. This was because early on, when I returned transcripts to participants, they frequently expressed alarm at the way their spoken contributions appeared when written verbatim. It did not seem fair for me to include interview data in a way which might cause discomfort to those who had contributed it (Wolcott 1994). With this proviso, I have tried to remain faithful to what participants said and to present, as far as possible, an account which is clear, but not 'sanitised' (Lather and Smithers, 1997, p. xvii).

I have presented participants' stories in a way which is clearly distinguishable from my own analysis, rather than selecting quotations to illustrate the points I wish to make. I hope that in doing so, readers can judge for themselves whether my interpretation is drawn from the data, rather from than my own preconceptions. Finally, I have been forced, for reasons of space and readability, to concentrate on the stories and descriptions of only a few of the participants, particularly those who did eventually move on to higher education. In doing so, I am aware that there is another story to be recounted: the story of those who did not take the path to higher education.

PROFILES OF THE PARTICIPANTS

Participants are listed in the order in which they were interviewed

Cycle one: individual interviews: building profiles of non-traditional students

1. June: 35 years old. A British woman of African-Caribbean origin. She has three school-aged children. June trained as a computer operator and worked as administrator and school secretary. She gave up work to pursue studies full-time. After a brief spell studying with Reachout, she undertook an Open University technology course, an access to teacher training course at a local further education college and an accountancy course at a local university. She did not pass the Open University exam and did not re-sit.

2. Carol: 29 years old. A British woman of African-Caribbean origin, who lives with her 11-year-old daughter. Carol left school at 16 and did a Youth Training Scheme in a department store, although she wanted to be a secretary. She completed a diploma in office skills and worked as a secretary until giving up her job to undertake further education. She started an access to social science course at a local further education college, with a view to going into social work. She approached Reach-out for advice about her career and education, and for study skills help with her college work.

3. Jane: A 42-year-old white British woman, who is married with two school-aged children. She attended a girls' grammar school which became a comprehensive. Jane left school after taking O-Levels and worked as a veterinary assistant. She completed a lay reader's course with her church. She considered further education in computing or languages and approached Reachout for advice.

4. Dave: A white British man, aged 34. Dave left school at 16. He had a negative experience of school, particularly because of problems with his English teacher and undiagnosed dyslexia. He went to a local further education college to study engineering. He worked in engineering and youth work. Dave considered returning to education when illness meant that he could no longer work in his former employment. He approached Reachout for advice.

5. *Pauline:* A 36-year-old woman of African-Caribbean origin. Pauline was frequently unable to attend school because of family responsibilities and she left school at 16 without qualifications. She undertook a college course in catering and worked on her English skills. She worked in catering. She started a part-time access course at a local college, but was unable to combine the course with her long working hours. She then began a Social Science access course with Reachout. Pauline was accepted to do an Open University course in health and social welfare starting in 1998. She started the course, but was unable to continue, due to lack of time, as she was doing two jobs. She went back to studying with Reachout and then restarted her Open University course. Illness prevented her from taking her first year examination and so she failed the course.

6. *Derek:* A 50-year-old white British man, who is married with two grown up children. He describes his secondary education as 'Victorian'. Derek had to leave school without taking his exams because of the death of his mother. He worked in the restaurant business and in social work. He returned to education when forced to rethink his future after a serious accident. He contacted Reachout for advice and applied and was accepted to do an access course, which he successfully completed. Illness prevented him from continuing study or work.

7. *Maria:* A 30-year-old white British woman with two young children. She was unable to attend school regularly because of family responsibilities. Maria left school at 15 without qualifications. She did a number of short courses and is active in her local community. She became a Reachout student for a term, but found the work too stressful. Maria still aims to return to education and would like to do social work or advice work.

8. *Harminder:* A 25-year-old British woman of Asian origin. Married with three small children. Harminder attended grammar school in London and left with A-Levels. She decided not to go on to college or university, but worked and travelled instead, until marrying and having a family. She attended a short parent volunteer course before joining a Reachout study group and then moving on to begin a Social Science degree with the Open University. She has successfully completed her fourth year of Open University study and is now working full time as a pupil mentor in a secondary school.

9. Laura: A 32-year-old woman of African-Caribbean origin. Laura has two school-aged children. She left school after taking CSEs and began as a youth trainee in catering. She worked in retailing until the birth of her first child and later enrolled on a nursery nursing course which she completed successfully. Laura now works as a play-scheme organiser. She was a Reachout home study student for some time. Laura is still unsure of what she wants to do educationally, but has considered applying to do teaching.

10. Siobhan: A 25-year-old white British woman. Siobhan has one school-aged daughter. She did not gain as good GCSE grades as she had hoped, because of a prolonged absence from school when she was thirteen. Siobhan narrowly missed gaining a place at college. She worked in a factory, then undertook an access course at a local further education college. She successfully completed the course, but was unsure what to do next. She started an A-Level, but left after her daughter was ill and she lost her crèche place. Siobhan did a number of short courses and studied with Reachout for a term. She has stopped studying for the time being, but is doing voluntary childcare work. Is unsure what her next move will be.

11. Monica: A 38-year-old British woman of African-Caribbean origin. Monica left school at 16 with seven CSEs and worked as an office junior until she had her first child. She returned to college to study book-keeping and was also a voluntary youth worker. She started a degree in business and finance but left after a few months, feeling that it was not what she really wanted to do. Monica now works as a community advice worker. She studied with a Reachout study group to prepare herself for undertaking an Open University course, but did not begin the course. Instead, she successfully gained a NVQ in careers guidance. She started an Open University course the following year, but did not complete. Interviewed twice.

12. Julie: A 40-year-old woman of African-Caribbean origin. Julie gained three GCSEs and one O-Level and left school at 17. She wanted to work with computers but was unable to do so at the time, as it involved a move to London, which her mother would not allow. Julie studied catering management at a local further education college, and worked in catering. She also brought up a family. She started two sociology courses at college, but was unable to finish because of her children's needs. She studied with Reachout for a short period and went on to complete a National Vocational Qualification in care.

13. Maureen: A 30-year-old white British woman, married with two small children. Maureen left school at 16. Her school experience was not a happy one, because she was bullied by other children. After leaving school, Maureen did a secretarial course at a local further education college, which she very much enjoyed. She worked in a number of secretarial jobs, leaving to have her two children, and then continued in part-time bar work. Her return to education was prompted by her involvement with a parent volunteer course. She studied with Reachout for a term, in a local study group and decided to pursue training as a crèche worker, which she has found deeply satisfying. Maureen is now qualified as a nursery worker.

14. Pamela: A 37-year-old woman of African-Caribbean origin. Pamela recently gave birth to her first child. She left school at sixteen without qualifications and worked in a factory, and then as a sales assistant. She attended a number of evening classes to improve her English skills, but felt that the classes and teachers offered her little help. Pamela studied with Reachout for a year. She stopped studying when she became pregnant, but plans to return to education.

15. Joy: A 38-year-old woman of African-Caribbean origin. Joy has two children of school age, and works as an integration assistant in a local school. She left school at 17, after taking GCEs. She went on to a local further education college to study for O-Levels. Joy decided to go back to college after her first child was born, and she was a volunteer at her nursery. She successfully completed a BTEC Diploma in nursery nursing. She worked first as a school parent link worker and then an integration assistant, and undertook a part-time introductory counselling course. She used Reachout for advice about what she could do next and how she could achieve her ambition to work in counselling or educational psychology. She was accepted to start a part-time Certificate of Higher Education in Psychology, which she completed successfully. **A speaker at *Students Speak* conference.**

16. Sue: A 38-year-old white British woman. Sue is married with four children, including five-year-old twins. She passed her 11-plus, but did not want to go to grammar school. She did not enjoy school at all, and left at 16. At that time, she wanted to do office work. She went to college to learn office and typing skills. After marrying and having her first child, Sue considered further study, but did not carry it through. She did a number of short parent volunteer courses, which built her confidence, and as a result, she became involved in a Reachout study group. She studied with a Reachout Access to Education group for a year, and went on to complete the first year of an Open University degree course. Sue started second year but withdrew. She undertook a part-time inservice course in education.

17. Jim: A 43-year-old white British man. Jim is married with four children of school age, the youngest of whom are twins. He gained six O-Level passes and went on to a local further education college to take A-Levels. He did not complete the course, but left to take a job in the Civil Service. He later ran his own successful business for a while. Jim had an undiagnosed dyslexia problem at school. It was not identified until he began a short integration assistant course, encouraged to do so by his wife and a friend. He had wanted to do an Open University course for some time. Jim joined a Reachout study group with his wife and friend, and applied to start an Open University degree the following year. Completed the first year. Started second year, but withdrew. **Helped with planning the *Students Speak* conference.**

Cycle two: individual interviews: developing relationships

18. Shilpa: A 30-year-old woman of Indian origin, married with three children, one of whom was born recently. Shilpa came to the UK when she was eleven. She had some unhappy memories of settling into school and particularly of studying maths. She left at the age of 16, unclear as to what she wanted to do. She trained as a nursery nurse, but was always keen to upgrade her qualifications. Shilpa studied part time at evening classes and completed the first module of an English degree. She worked as a home school liaison teacher and then a trainer in the local education authority. Shilpa was involved with Reachout both profes-sionally and as a maths student. She successfully completed her GCSE Maths with Reachout and completed two years of an Open University degree. Interviewed twice.

19. Nargis: A 21-year-old of Bangladeshi origin who was born and educated in Birmingham. Nargis had always wanted to go into teaching, but felt that she was poorly advised as to the best way to achieve her ambition. She was directed to vocational training, rather than academic study. After qualifying as a nursery nurse, Nargis became a nursery assistant in a local school. She still has an ambition to be a teacher. She began studying for her maths GCSE but did not complete. Gained a part-time City and Guilds adult teacher training certificate. Postponed the idea of teaching when she went to Bangladesh to marry.

20. Salma: A 30-year-old British woman of Pakistani origin, Salma has two children under eight, whom she brings up single-handed. She did well at school, but left shortly after starting her A-Level course when she went to Pakistan to marry. After divorcing, she returned to education, with her family's support. She completed Reachout's social science Access Course in six months and gained a place at university to study social policy. Salma successfully completed her studies. Interviewed twice. **A workshop leader at the *Students Speak* conference.**

21. Paul: A 45-year-old white man. He has two children. Paul was in the bottom class at school, classified as a slow learner. He is not sure whether he is dyslexic, but this seems quite likely. He was not entered for any examinations and left school without qualifications. Paul went to work in the building trade, and then as a driver. He returned to education in his mid-twenties when he decided to learn French. He also attended basic skills classes and then started studying with Reachout. Began the first year of an Open University degree course but did not complete it.

22. Donna: A 30-year-old British woman of African-Caribbean origin. Donna left school at 16 with CSEs. She started an A-Level course at college, but left after a year. Later, she completed a full-time access course, and gained a place at university to study for a degree. Illness compelled her to leave during her third year, and she decided not to return. She started a Diploma in Social Work course, which she left because of money and housing problems, planning to return. On return, a back injury cause her to drop out again. She has now restarted her social work training. **Helped with planning the *Students Speak* conference.**

23. Ann: A 34-year-old white British woman who has a 6-year-old child. Ann gained O-Levels at school and planned to stay on for

A-Levels. However, the school's sixth form closed and she went to a local college to study theatre studies and English. Ann lost interest in her studies as she was actively pursuing a career in performance. On leaving college at the age of eighteen, she had gained her equity card, but done poorly in her A-Levels. She started an access course, but gave it up when she became pregnant. She started another course, but it did not suit her needs. When her child went to nursery, she decided to start studying again, and successfully gained a science GCSE. She completed Reachout Maths GCSE and started an Open University Science course but did not complete her first year.

24. Lee: A 28-year-old British man of African-Caribbean origin. He left school with relatively poor O-Level grades, which he improved at college the following year. Lee went on to do youth work in a variety of settings. He applied to college to do a Diploma in Community and Youth Work, but failed to gain a place. He then started an Access to community and youth work course, but did not complete it. Lee started studying with Reachout to prepare himself for another application to study youth and community work. He started an Open University course, but dropped out quite quickly. He was accepted to study part-time for a youth and community work qualification. Dropped out after one year. Now studying full-time for a degree, with a view to becoming a teacher.

25. Sara: Sara is a 30-year-old woman of English and Pakistani heritage. She has six children. She left sixth form college with GCSEs and went on to start A-Levels. Family responsibilities forced her to give up full-time study. Marriage and childcare meant that she had to go to work to support her family. She also did voluntary work as an English teacher. Joined a Reachout study group and gained access credits. Then she found a new job. She still plans to train as a social worker eventually.

26. Patricia: A 36-year-old British woman of African-Caribbean origin, who has four children. The youngest is a year old. Patricia left school at 16 with GCSEs and went on to do a social care course at college. She gave up the course when she was expecting her first child. She went on to start another access course and to complete a secretarial course. She could not continue her studies because she needed to work to support her children. Patricia worked as a care assistant but decided to return to study to gain a social work qualification and improve her prospects. She studied with a local Reachout group and gained a place on a Diploma in Social Work course. She has successfully completed her second year and is working as a social worker. **Speaker at *Students Speak* conference.**

27. Helen: A 40-year-old woman of Jamaican origin, who was educated in the UK from the age of eight. She has four children, the youngest being three. Helen felt that her education suffered because of attitudes to black children at that time. She also felt that she received little support in her education from either her family or careers advisors. She left school at 16 with CSEs and did a number of jobs, married and brought up a family. Helen returned to education, via a Reachout study group and was accepted to study full-time for a Diploma in Social Work. She completed the course successfully and is now a Social Worker. **Speaker at *Students Speak* conference.**

28. Ruth: Jamaican-born and educated in the UK from the age of nine. At school, Ruth had a sense of being 'different' because of her origins. She left home at 15 and was briefly in care. She was therefore unable to take her CSEs and left school without qualifications. She trained as a waitress, and became a dancer and model in the UK and Germany. She returned to education after learning German and undertaking a beauty therapy course in Germany. Was unable to complete course because she did not have previous qualifications. Ruth returned to the UK and qualified as a beauty therapist but did not feel fulfilled. She spent some time seeking an educational direction. Studied with Reachout to prepare herself for entry to higher education. Studied part-time for a Certificate of Higher Education in psychology and completed the course successfully. **Speaker at *Students Speak* conference.**

29. Jacqui: A 29-year-old British woman of African-Caribbean origin, Jacqui has a 9-year-old daughter. She was an 'average' student, but felt distanced from other pupils at her school. She left with four GCSEs and went to college to do a City and Guilds course in Community Care. She went back to college to do Maths and English and then studied for a BTEC in Social Care. The birth of her daughter prevented her starting work for a year, but she studied counselling part time, and became a nursery officer when her daughter was one. Jacqui had a bad experience when she did a second counselling course and this deterred her from continuing study for some time. After attending a Reachout residential weekend, she decided to apply to do a full-time Diploma in Social Work course. Successfully completed the course and is now a social worker. **Speaker at *Students Speak* conference.**

30. Seima: A 27-year-old British woman of Pakistani origin. Seima has two children under 5, whom she has raised single-handed since she was divorced from her husband. Educated to GCSE level, she also undertook a college course in business studies. Seima returned to study through Reachout and successfully gained her Access Certificate. She applied for and was accepted to study for a degree in childhood studies. She has now graduated. Interviewed twice. **Speaker at *Students Speak* conference.**

Cycle three: individual interviews: the first year in higher education

11. Monica: Interviewed for a second time, after failing to complete the first year of an Open University degree.

18. Shilpa: Interviewed for a second time at the end of her first year on Open University study.

27. Helen: Interviewed for a second time, at the end of her first year studying for a Diploma in Social Work. **Speaker at the *Students Speak* Conference.**

31. Gloria: A 34-year-old black British woman; the mother of two small children, one under six months. Gloria gained a BTEC diploma in nursery nursing. She decided to apply to study at degree level after attending a Reachout residential course. She went on to study full time for a degree in childhood studies, which she successfully completed. Gloria aims eventually to become a teacher. **Report reader for the *Students Speak* conference.**

32. Janet: A 36-year-old woman of dual heritage. Janet is the mother of two children, one of school age. She worked as a part-time adult educator. Janet held a business studies qualification and an adult teaching certificate. She felt that she was stuck in her career and undertook an Open University degree level course. She completed the course successfully, but failed the final exam. She decided not to re-sit the exam when she gained a job as a teacher in Jamaica. **Speaker at *Students Speak* conference.**

33. Baljit: A 29-year-old British woman of Indian origin. She is a mother of a five-year-old daughter. Baljit left school at 16 with GCSEs. She decided to return to education and studied for her Access Certificate with Reachout. She applied and was accepted to study full time for a degree in English. She has successfully completed her degree and is now training to be a teacher.

34. Jenny: A 32-year-old British woman of African-Caribbean origin and mother of a five-year-old daughter. Jenny completed a number of short courses, including a parent volunteer course and two modules of a part-time higher education certificate. She applied for, and was accepted to study for a youth and community work qualification. She successfully passed the first year in spite of a prolonged period of serious illness. Did not return for the second year of her course.

35. Sandra: A 36-year-old woman of African-Caribbean origin. Sandra is the mother of three children, including twins. She worked in administration, studied part-time for an NVQ in business administration and was a probation service volunteer. She wanted to become a social worker but did not have the requisite qualification. After studying an Access to social science course with Reachout, Sandra was accepted to study full time for a diploma in social work. She is now qualified and working as a social worker. She is completing the final year of her degree on a part-time basis. **Speaker at *Students Speak* conference.**

36. Hazel: A 40-year-old British woman of African-Caribbean origin. Hazel is a mother of two children. Active in her community for a number of years, she undertook an access to social science course. She then started an Open University course, but was unable to cope with the pressure of work. She applied for and was accepted to study full time for a youth and community work qualification. Successfully gained her professional qualification and gained a degree in social science. Now working full time as a community and youth worker in the area where she lives.

37. Caroline: A 28-year-old British woman of African-Caribbean origin. Caroline is qualified as a nursery nurse. She wanted to go into teaching, but was unable to progress because of her need to work full time. Caroline completed a degree with the Open University and studied maths with Reachout. She went on to complete a part-time university course in music and education. **Speaker at *Students Speak* conference.**

Part One

TALKING ABOUT EDUCATION

2

SCHOOLDAYS:
STORIES OF FRUSTRATION

I wanted to know so much
Pauline: REACHOUT participant

This chapter records some of the participants' perceptions of their school lives, their memories of themselves as school students and of their teachers. The interviews I carried out with students at this stage were aimed at gaining information about their educational backgrounds and aspirations; what had prevented them continuing their education in the past and what had motivated their return to education. I was interested to know how they remembered school life: had they harboured particular ambitions when they were at school, had they enjoyed their schooldays, had they failed crucial exams? I was also interested to know whether and how they had been advised about possible post-school education and career options.

I had made certain initial assumptions about why participants had not had the opportunity to study at higher education level earlier in life. The first, influenced by the ethnographic literature about class, race, gender and schooling (Willis 1977, Mac an Ghaill 1989, Woods 1990, Wright 1993) was that participants would recall either disaffection from, or resistance to school, resulting from a sense of exclusion from the norms and expectations of a white, middle class, male oriented educational system. The second, informed by 'barriers' explanations of non-participation (Cross 1981, Woodley *et al* 1987, McGivney 1990) was that institutional, situational and dispositional barriers stood in the way of educational motivation and progress. The interviews revealed a slightly more complex picture. It showed the students as engaged in a long-term struggle to reach educational goals, frequently impeded by barriers of lack of interest, lack of information and lack of guidance from those who might have been expected to support them. It revealed them not as disaffected but as remarkably committed to finding a way forward.

Schooldays

What was striking in the accounts of the participants' schooldays was their description of their performance at school as average and, with a few notable exceptions, as consistent in their attendance. However, there were some recurrent themes in their initial descriptions of their experiences. These revealed that although their schooldays may have been viewed with hindsight as uneventful, there were aspects of school experience which led participants to feel that higher education was not something to which they could aspire, and that their futures lay in vocational training, early entry to the job market or (in the case of a number of the women) marriage and family life, immediately after leaving school. Factors which they described as having an impact on their education included:

– the experience of difference

– lack of information and support from family

– difficulties with schooling

– having limited choices

These factors, which often interacted, seemed to reveal a picture not of disaffected non-participants at school but of frustrated participants, motivated to succeed educationally, but unable to do so. This picture of frustrated participation seemed to carry on beyond schooldays and into adult life, as participants attempted to find an educational and career direction.

SCHOOLDAYS – THE EXPERIENCE OF DIFFERENCE
Put at the back: Helen's story

Helen had her initial education in Jamaica, and began her schooling in England in the early seventies, when she was 11. As a black child in a small Midlands town, she was very much in the minority, one of only fifteen black children in a school of around two hundred pupils. She felt that she had come to the country with a good educational background, and that she had already covered some of the work she was expected to do at her new school:

> We were put at the back of the class, sort of thing. I remember that distinctly. So I just learnt what I could. But we weren't concentrated on like the rest of the kids. And at that time, you just don't know how to do anything about it. Now you do because you've got all this legislation and you know your rights and so on. But then, you just had to. Plus it was a small town. So it was even worse.

Helen gained a strong sense of being different and, in particular, of being treated differently from other pupils because of differences in language:

> I learned more when I was in Jamaica, from about the age of five, than here. Most of the things that I was learning when I was at primary school, I'd already learnt them. But, because we speak a patois, you can imagine, they found it hard to understand me, and I found it hard to understand them until about a year afterwards. Then – because of that – back of the class again . . . They ignored you, because they could not communicate. And I was there, trying to think: What's she saying? Some words – they were basically the same words – but it took six months to a year before I realised what they were actually saying. Because, don't forget, where I'm coming from, it's English, but it's very broken. At one stage, they brought in some sort of English teacher; and he sort of specialised with the black and Asian children. But it wasn't anything in depth. Actually, it was just putting them at the back of the class and doing something 'low' with them. It wasn't helping them . . . I learnt a few things, but not what I wanted to learn. They kept you back. If you speak to all the girls that were in my class, they'll tell you the same thing. We had to leave town because it was – oh, it was really difficult. You could go to college, but again, you were pushed to the back of the class. You'd have to really excel to actually be noticed.

Helen was led to believe that her 'broken English' gave her difficulties throughout her educational life, including later at university when she was training to become a social worker.

Being 'different': Ruth's story

Ruth came from rural Jamaica to join her mother at the age of nine. She describes her schooling in the Caribbean:

> We were very poor. I'm not ashamed to say this. Very poor. The school was a long way from home and they didn't have buses allocated for school children like you do here. People went to school when you could afford it. You had to buy everything for school. If you had no lunch money, you couldn't go to school, because you would either faint from the sun or die of thirst. So you went to school occasionally. I think when I came here, I was behind in my schooling. I was certainly behind in telling the time, and I remember my mother – most evenings I used to dread it, because the clock would come out, and I'd get a clout every time I said a wrong word. That was just their way, you know. I don't suppose you could do that now. Yes, I was behind, and my reading was poor. But I loved reading so I soon caught up.

Ruth made friends at school, in spite of her early homesickness. However, she felt that her Jamaican accent marked her out:

> I don't think I got on well with the teachers. I think maybe because I was Jamaican. I still had a very strong West Indian accent at that time, so it would have been difficult. I did feel different – I felt different. There were other black children there as well at the school. But I think I felt different because I spoke with a strong West Indian accent at the time. And not only that; I think that most teachers were – probably a middle class background. That would probably be different for them as well, and made them a little uncertain how to adjust to me. But I didn't feel I couldn't adjust. If more interest was taken, probably it would have been better . . . I think that [teachers] felt that a lot of black children were no-hopers. I don't quite know why. If you had an attitude, or if you had any sort of assertiveness at all – which I think should belong to all people of colour or whatever you are – I think you should have some sort of substance about you. But I think, if you did, as a black person, you were sort of 'marked' by it. If you were subdued and you were sort of 'yes sir, yes miss' – not known to have an opinion, you were left alone to get on.

Tension at home meant that Ruth ran away at the age of fifteen. She was admitted to care for a while. By the time she returned to school, she had missed her exams:

When I went back to school, it was just before they broke up. So I missed out on my exams. I think to myself, something could have been done about that. But it wasn't done, and I don't know why. I thought I couldn't stay on, because everyone I knew would have been gone. So I didn't stop on. I felt a bit of a prat. I wasn't encouraged to. No one told me I could.

Ruth eventually went on to study for a degree in psychology.

The language barrier: Shilpa's story

Shilpa went to primary school in India, where she was born. She stressed the difference between her experience and that of other pupils:

I don't think mine is a normal, usual case because I came from India at the age of eleven. So rather than having the primary background of this country, I went straight into the second year with very little English language. So my experience of secondary school wasn't a very happy one.

Reflecting on her unhappiness, Shilpa particularly recalled her problems with learning maths:

I wasn't very happy, because I felt I wasn't learning anything, due to the language. I wasn't learning maths particularly. I was very good at maths in India but, because of the transition, the language barrier, I felt completely lost in maths, and I felt I wasn't learning science, I wasn't learning history – I wasn't understanding history, science and geography. And I didn't understand. My understanding did build up, but not to the level that I would have wanted to, looking back now.

In spite of her unhappiness, and without even studying the syllabus, Shilpa gained a good grade in Punjabi, along with art and social science. She was motivated to succeed, but was unable to do so because of her problems with language at that time.

I did Punjabi GCSE. Just the exam was offered, and I took it without studying the syllabus. I had a grade B for that. But at that time it wasn't considered important, so I didn't think much of it.

Looking back, she felt she could have been helped through this period:

I think somebody – a very understanding teacher who spoke my language and who understood me – would have helped me at that time – who could translate to me the concepts of learning. I didn't have that, at that time.

Shilpa left school immediately after taking her GCSEs, and did not go into further education until four years later, after her marriage:

I was happy, very happy to leave school.

She eventually trained as a nursery worker, worked as a home-school liaison officer, brought up three children and went on to study for a Master's Degree with the Open University.

The experience of difference

Most of the participants in the study who were of African-Caribbean, South Asian or Irish origin were born in Britain or had all their education in this country. Ruth, Helen, and Shilpa were exceptions. Their initial education took place in the country of their birth – Jamaica in the case of Ruth and Helen and India in Shilpa's case. However, their arrival in the English school system left them feeling inadequate and different from their classmates, on account of their background, language and culture.

These women all underwent secondary education before the Swann Report (1985) highlighted the consistent disadvantage experienced by children from ethnic minorities. Since then, there have been a number of ethnographic studies directed towards uncovering the relationship between ethnic minority pupils, their teachers and school organisation. Some of these (for example Mac an Ghaill 1989, Wright 1993) have described the formation of counter-school cultures among pupils in reaction to their experience of racism and their sense of marginalisation from school ethos and aims. Cecile Wright (1993) observed that pupils of African-Caribbean and to some extent, Asian origin were more likely to be placed in lower streams than their white counterparts. She highlighted the way in which African-Caribbean pupils were subjected to teachers' racist stereotypes and, in some cases, to overtly racist treatment. Wright went on to describe the formation of an anti-school sub-culture as a response to this. Peter Woods (1990) calls this process differentiation-polarization:

> ... academic differentiation by the school will lead to a polarization of
> sub-cultures among pupils, between those championing pro-school
> and those anti-school values. (Woods 1990, p. ix)

The stories of school life told by Ruth, Helen and Shilpa give the impression that pupils coming from backgrounds other than white and British felt that they were viewed with caution and distance by their teachers; that they were either marked out as difficult (as in Ruth's case) or (as in the case of Helen and Shilpa) that they were left to get on pretty much on their own. However, their stories did not reveal them as having anti-school attitudes or as participating in anti-school sub-cultures. On the contrary, they seemed to remain quite committed to education both whilst at school and afterwards. Whilst there did appear to have been differentiation, the polarisation theory did not seem to hold.

The linguistic marginalisation of students from working class backgrounds, fed by theories of restricted linguistic code (Bernstein 1973), has been discussed by Gillian Plummer (2000). Drawing on her own experiences and those of other women from working class backgrounds, she describes how working class ways of speaking are often labelled as deficient. The linguistic marginalisation of pupils from ethnic minorities has also been noted. Moore (1993), describing his study of some of the assumptions and practices involved in bilingual teaching and learning, reveals the way in which bilingual teaching, whilst aiming to encourage children's expression and writing in English, may fail to acknowledge the validity of bilingual pupils' everyday life experiences and backgrounds and their pre-existing learning conventions in favour of those conventions which are assumed as superior in UK schools. This assumption of cultural and linguistic superiority that is embedded in the education system has been described as symbolic violence (Bourdieu 1977, Bourdieu and Passeron 1977):

> . . . the imposition of a cultural arbitrary by an arbitrary power.
> (Bourdieu and Passeron 1977, p. 5)

It seems that, for Helen, Ruth and Shilpa, struggling with their newcomer status in British schools at the age of eleven, symbolic violence was done to their concept of themselves as learners, linguists and as people with a strong cultural, historic and linguistic heritage.

SCHOOLDAYS – FAMILY INFORMATION AND SUPPORT
No-one advised me: Siobhan's story

Siobhan was of Irish origin and had come to England when she was a small child. She had been successful academically until a family crisis kept her away from school for a prolonged period at the age of 13. This, she felt, affected her GCSE grades:

> I took all of my GCSEs, and I passed all of them, but my highest grade, I guess, was a C. I missed a lot of time at school; I missed most of the third year, and when I went back, I was determined to catch up what I'd missed . . . because previously I'd been a straight A's student. I just sort of went haywire at thirteen. I was getting myself back to being a B student, which was pretty good, considering I'd missed a year.

Siobhan received a mixed reception on her return to school:

> The deputy headmistress, she was OK with me at first. Then, once I went into the classroom, it was as if I didn't exist. Some of the teachers' attitudes were: you've missed a year; carry on – I don't know what your attitude is yet. But some of them were really encouraging. One particular teacher was absolutely brilliant; she took time to talk to me and say: if there's anything you need to talk to me about, inside or outside school . . . I desperately wanted to learn and I desperately wanted to catch up. There was one particular teacher . . . I was in her English class. And I think it was in the first couple of months back, and I think she was trying to put me in my place, to say right, knuckle down, or I don't want to know you.

In Siobhan's case, being absent seemed to constitute grounds to suspect anti-school attitudes which, in turn, meant unsuitability to progress. In spite of her setbacks, she remained committed to school and to going on to college after she left school:

> I was never in any sort of bad trouble – fighting or anything like that. And I always had something to say in class. For the most part, I was shown respect by teachers, and I'd show them respect. One thing I always had throughout school was respect for the teachers.

Siobhan's father had come to England as a young man. As a lone parent, he had worked hard to support his family, but lacked the experience of how the education system worked to help his daughter forward. He was proud of her achievements at school but was unable to help her overcome a fairly minor educational setback:

And I actually did get a place at college, depending on whether I got a B in English. And my Dad was always very proud of me, you know. And I went along, got the interview, and the interview was fine. And my Dad was so proud of me: the first one of the Moores to go to college. And so the offer of this place – this was for a childcare course – was provisional on a B in English. And I didn't get a B in English, so I couldn't take the course. I mean, even then, no one advised me and said: if you want to, you can go back and get a B in English, and you can come back next year.

Nobody ever said it was important: Sue's story

Sue was of Irish origin, born in England to a working class family. She did well in her early years at school, and passed her 11-plus examination. However, she had no wish to go on to the grammar school:

I passed my 11-plus. I passed my art exam as well. So I had the choice of art school and the local grammar school as well. I didn't come from a very supportive family. So I wanted to go where my friends were going – to the local comp [comprehensive school].

She went to the comprehensive school, but was placed in the Grammar School stream – separated from her friends. She felt out of place in the top stream:

I didn't like school. I hated school. I mean, I was good. I was good at maths; I enjoyed maths . . . about the only supportive teacher I had. Because I was one of the scruffy kids. The ones they don't really bother about.

Sue was not encouraged educationally at home, either:

Nobody ever said it was important; education's important. There was just nothing. No support from anywhere – from the family; not even really from school.

Sue went on to study with the Open University.

We didn't have role models: Pamela's story

Pamela's parents came from Jamaica when she was small. She spent part of her primary, and all of her secondary schooling in England. She felt that her teachers did not understand the needs of black children:

They [teachers] didn't know how to take us, our attitudes, our parents – us. They don't want to adapt. They've been through their courses, but they haven't taken on board ethnic minorities . . . you just sit there, be quiet; do this and that, and that's it.

Pamela did not take GCSEs. She felt she was not given the chance to do so, and that a combination of lack of parental support and lack of teacher support meant that black children could not progress education-ally in the 1970s:

In them days, our mothers didn't have time for us, and these days, we've got time. Because we don't want to see what happened to us happen to our kids . . . We won't let our kids go through the same system. So the teachers have got to be there. Besides, they're getting paid for it. If they don't want to do the job, why be there?

She felt that pupils like herself lacked role models who could encourage their educational progress:

Being at school, we didn't have role models. There was no Chinese, no Indian doctors, no black teachers, not at all.

Family information and support

Most of the participants were educated entirely in Britain, in city schools. In the main, they did not recall a sense of isolation similar to that which the newcomers to the British school system reported. A considerable number, however, felt that their parents' relationship to the school system had held them back educationally. They felt disadvantaged by their parents' outsider status and their lack of knowledge about the British education system.

Family circumstances affected participants' views of how they had progressed at school. Siobhan, Pauline and Maria had all sustained periods of absence from school. Sara, Laura and Derek were forced to leave school early because of the illness or death of a parent. They shared a sense of regret and of opportunities missed. Whilst Siobhan felt that her father would have helped her, had he known how, Sue, Pauline and Pamela did not feel encouraged by their families, who did not see the value of education as a means to a future career.

Reay (1998) has discussed parents', and particularly mothers' role in helping their primary school children to accrue cultural capital (Bourdieu 1997). The availability of time, information, knowledge and the ability to be assertive in relation to the education system appear to be important factors in enabling children to benefit from it, and ultimately, accrue economic capital. Reay concludes that migrancy, and in particular the experience of being educated outside Britain, is likely to affect the extent to which parents can access the benefits of education for their own children. Plummer (2000) has also described the family pressures which keep girls from working class backgrounds from developing their educational aspirations. A number of the women in this study experienced similar pressures, being expected to fill the domestic place of absent or sick mothers, or to become economically active as soon as possible, to improve the family's economic situation. Family circumstances, coupled with structured inequality of access to information and support (Reay 1998), meant that they could not use the education system to their advantage.

SCHOOLDAYS – DIFFICULTIES WITH SCHOOLING
Missing school: Pauline's story

Pauline is of black British origin. She was one of six children. She described there being only one book in the house when she was a child – *The Owl and the Pussycat* – which she read avidly, over and again. At school, Pauline remembered her teachers, lessons and other pupils fondly. However, family commitments kept her away from school for long spells :

> Lovely school; I loved going there. But because of family problems I was not able to go because my mom kept me at home to look after her and the family. So they said I wouldn't be able to sit any exams because I went in one day a week and that's all. So I didn't have much education. I loved school. The teachers were very good and supportive and the pupils were great.

In spite of her happy memories, it seems that the difficulties she was experiencing in attending school, and the reasons for non-attendance, were not picked up:

> But if you had problems in education . . . they didn't look at that side of it; they didn't ask students why. I had ill health and asthma, but that wasn't a problem. It didn't stop me from going to school. My mom used it as a problem . . . The teachers didn't think – well, why is this person missing school, is there a background reason? They assume you are just wagging it . . . But I knew in the back of my

mind that if they had seen the alarm signals, they could have got me out of the situation. Because I went in and explained to one of the teachers, that I was having problems at home. But she just said: 'your mum is a nice woman'.

Pauline describes herself as a quiet pupil, but one who enjoyed going to school:

Yes, a very quiet pupil. I think it was because I was never in school. And you know, too, how West Indian parents say that you must be seen and not heard. So that's the reason I was quiet. I wasn't allowed to speak up for myself.

Later in life, while she was studying sociology, Pauline reflected on her school experience as a black person. She could relate to some of the discussions about why black children were classified as 'under-achievers' in school:

When they talk about black people and education. Well, I didn't know it was down on paper like that. Yes, it exists, and I've seen it in me . . . It was one of them that said black children are more shy. Too afraid to speak. And I was like that at school. I always kept quiet . . . There's just some things you don't talk about, do you?

Pauline went on to study with the Open University.

Shyness or slowness: Paul's story

Paul's parents came from Ireland during the Second World War. Both his parents were unable to read and write, and they worked in jobs which did not entail their being able to demonstrate these skills:

My Mother can't spell at all. She can just about write her own name in a way. She worked in a factory. And my father – his spelling looks a bit dyslexic to be honest. So there wouldn't be any parent back-up at all, while I was at school. They did encourage me in a way. They'd say you were doing well, because to them, if I wrote something, I was doing well . . . My father was a painter and decorator, and my mother worked in a factory. So neither of them had to use any academic skills. So I sort of followed in their footsteps. And I think, because of shyness or slowness, it was taking me time.

Paul left school at fifteen without qualifications. All he took from school was his last school report, which gave him 'C' grades in all his subjects, and indicated, variously that he: 'lacked concentration' was 'average', 'untidy' and 'satisfactory'. The concept of dyslexia was not commonly known when Paul was at school:

> I wouldn't have heard of the word myself then . . . My schooldays are a bit hazy in terms of people actually helping. No teacher stands out as coming up to me and saying: Well, all right, you've got a problem . . . I remember some teachers who were boring, and the one method the maths teacher had: if you didn't know your times table, you would get the stick on your hand. So I can't remember my times tables either, to this day. It's just blocked. I can't remember it.

He was in the lowest class – class 4E – but did not realise the significance of this until later:

> It was later on I realised what level I was. You know, when you're going through, I don't remember thinking whatever caused me to be that level, whether it was dyslexia or because I was shy, sitting at the back. I don't really know.

Paul got a job as a plumber's mate immediately after leaving school and carried on working, without further education, until he was 21 and decided to learn to drive:

> I think I was still a shy type of person. So the level of education was holding me back in that sense. But I don't think I really appreciated it in that period. Just carried on working, and didn't get a trade at all really. Until I was twenty-one. Somebody asked me if I could drive, and I started driving and I've been basically driving ever since.

Paul moved on from learning to drive to learning French. Then, recognising for himself his reading, writing and memory difficulties, he started basic skills education, taking on maths and English and eventually studying with the Open University.

Isolated: Jacqui's story

Jacqui's family was of Jamaican origin, but she was born and educated in England. Jacqui's mother died when she was young. She described herself as being 'very isolated' at school but she nursed a strong desire from childhood to work with people:

> I can remember when I was young wanting to be a nurse; every child wants to be a nurse. I just felt as though I had a personality

where I like being around people. And that probably had to do with me being quite a lonely child.

She did not enjoy secondary school and was bullied by other pupils:

I didn't get on with a lot of the other people of my age. All the teachers loved me; That's probably why nobody else liked me. And that was because I'd grown up on my own. I was choosy about who I wanted to be with. They probably took it as a negative. I was very mature for my age. I never felt that there was a point in my schooling where I was encouraged into saying: this is the direction I'm going.

Pushed aside: Maureen's story

Maureen was of white British origin. She gained two O-Levels at school. She felt that she would have done better if she had not been treated badly by her classmates:

I don't know if it was so much the school itself, as the class I was in. I tended to be excluded from everything and pushed aside. Sort of bullying, if you like. I was made to feel down. I was made to feel inferior to everyone else. Of course, I never said anything about it . . . if I had done, maybe something could have been sorted out. I think I'd have been happier. I would have achieved a lot more.

On leaving school she went to college to do a secretarial course. She enjoyed and was active in college life:

There was a student union there, and I was chosen to be the rep for my class. And that was wonderful; having to attend meetings and reporting back the next day.

In spite of being happy at college, however, Maureen felt that her isolation at school had affected her prospects:

If things had been different then, I would have succeeded.

Difficulties with schooling

One striking aspect in the educational recollections of the small number of men interviewed was the extent to which dyslexia featured in their stories. Of the five, three – Paul, Dave and Jim – reported learning difficulties which were not addressed at school. Paul, who had been in a remedial class all his school life, was unaware of the implications of this for his future prospects until much later. Compared to his parents, who could not read either, and to his classmates who also had learning difficulties, he had felt he was an 'average' pupil. Dave, however, felt keenly the stigma attached to dyslexia and had clear and bitter memories of being picked on by teachers because of his reading difficulties. Jim's writing and reading problems seemed to go more or less unnoticed at school. Time and again, he re-sat and failed examinations. He left school and went to college but, again, felt out of his depth and gave up studying for a number of years. His problem was not identified until much later in life, when he attended an adult education class.

None of the women interviewed reported learning difficulties at school and none identified themselves as dyslexic. Research into the incidence of dyslexia indicates that it is more common among boys than girls (Huston 1992). There seems to be little consensus about the reasons for this. What is clear, however, is that the effects of dyslexia that goes unrecognised or misrecognised can be serious. Janice Edwards (1994) has explored the world of dyslexic boys and reveals a picture of educational careers marked by teacher and pupil bullying, neglect and humiliation. The effects of these experiences on the boys she studied included loss of confidence, truancy and social isolation. Edwards also notes that people with dyslexia tend to develop a strong sense of survival, coupled with an enthusiasm which requires encouragement, rather than marginalisation and discrimination. This enthusiasm was apparent in the men interviewed. They were keen to take on work challenges and, once their reading and writing problems were addressed, they were eager to take on educational challenges as well.

Although none of the women in this study reported being dyslexic, a number of them did experience problems at school. Maureen and Jacqui were bullied by other children. Both had been quiet and conscientious pupils, with early career ambitions which were dependent on gaining good examination results. Both had been isolated and picked on by classmates. Ann experienced a year of bullying, not from fellow pupils but at the hands of her teacher.

Studies of bullying in school (Olweus 1993, Tattum 1993, Tattum and Herbert 1993, Rigby 1997) have tended to concentrate on defining bullying, identifying what makes a bully and developing strategies for managing bullying. There has been little research which examines the effects of bullying at school on educational progress. However, Rigby (1997) has drawn attention to the likelihood that it may lead to low self-esteem, increased social isolation, absenteeism and poor health. The effects of bullying on Maureen, Jacqui and Ann were that it held them back educationally and sapped their confidence while they were at school. Maureen and Ann felt that they recovered to some extent but Jacqui lived in fear of being picked on throughout her educational career. Indeed she was, this time by a college tutor. She therefore anticipated university entry with considerable trepidation, fearing that the pattern would repeat itself.

Difficulties at school which were beyond the control of participants seemed to go unnoticed by teachers or even to be caused by teachers. From the point of view of a number of the participants, such treatment held back their educational and work careers. The fact that Jim, Paul, Jacqui and Ann eventually managed to go on to study successfully at higher education level is testament to their determination. Had they been given support at school, it is likely that they would have made educational progress earlier in their lives.

SCHOOLDAYS – FRUSTRATED CHOICES
In the wrong place: Ann's story

Ann was of white British origin. She described her secondary schooling as sexist:

> It was definitely quite sexist. One term girls would do needlework, and one term they would do cookery. Nobody ever asked us: would you fancy having a go? Lads would do woodwork or metalwork. Maybe some of the lads would like to have done cookery, but nobody asked them either.

Ann suffered bullying at the hands of a teacher:

> One year, there was a teacher who bullied me for no good reason. This was when I was about 8 or 9. I think it knocks the stuffing out of you. It sets you back maybe two, three years. Just silly things, like humiliating me; sitting me next to children who had behaviour problems; or sitting me next to windows that were open in winter; kicking your bag around the room; or making you write in pencil – you know.

She was in the top stream at secondary school. Nevertheless, she had problems with taking O-Levels, rather than the lower graded CSEs:

> I had to fight quite hard to do some of my O-Levels They trained you up to do CSEs, because they didn't want you to waste public money by coming out with nothing. But I insisted. I achieved an A in literature and a B in language. You had to do science, that was compulsory. So, typically, I chose human biology. A lot of girls did that. They didn't choose physics or chemistry, and I don't think they were encouraged to. So I got an A in that. I was really proud of achieving those. I did music as well, but they only did a CSE in music, and I got CSE 2, which was disappointing.

Ann planned to stay on at school to do A-Levels, but she experienced further problems:

> I always seem to be in the wrong place, or the wrong age group at the wrong time. During my last year at secondary school, my head teacher called those of us in who wanted to stay on in the sixth form. We had a sixth form at that time. And he said, the Council are going to start abolishing sixth forms at certain schools, and we're one of them. So you are going to have to find somewhere else to go. So that was a bit of a shock to the system. Because I knew I was doing quite well. I had everything lined up in my mind: what A-Levels I was going to do. But I was told I couldn't stay on at school. So I had to find a college to go to. And then everything changed because they didn't do [the subjects] I wanted to do.

She left school, went to a college, but did not continue for long with her chosen subject:

> I think I was denied that. If I had a couple of decent A-Levels – then it would have been easier for me now.

Frustrated choices

Aside from the implicit gendered assumptions about girls' and boys' career paths and life chances (documented by, *inter alia*, Sharpe 1976, Delamont 1980, Spender 1982, Arnot and Weiner 1987, Measor and Sikes 1992), there were also ways in which options were closed down by seemingly arbitrary changes in school organisation, course availability and policy changes. For Ann, changes to school organisation in the sixth form threw her plans awry. Similarly, Jane was unable to follow her chosen career path when her school was amalgamated with another and lost its sixth form. Nargis, Laura and Carol were caught up in the move towards school-based vocational training which became prevalent in the eighties and nineties (Wickham 1986, Brown 1987). Nargis was steered towards childcare work, Laura towards catering, Carol towards shop work.

Participants experienced the closing down of options, often not realising this until later in life, when they tried to move on educationally or in their careers. They were not helped by a lack of information and advice on the value of qualifications. The choices they were supposed to have did not, in practice, seem to be genuine choices. Woods (1984) has discussed the 'myth' of subject choice at school, and the way that choice is subtly manipulated by the school and teachers. Subject choice is seen by Woods as a triangular process, involving teachers, parents and pupils, with teachers as key mediators within a framework of institutional channelling. At a macro level, the process is geared towards meeting society's, rather than the individual child's needs and at a micro level, it is geared towards exam success, rather than educational ends. If one adds to this the informational disadvantages which parents of these students had, the power of teachers and the school to guide 'choice' becomes even greater.

In the case of a number of the participants in this study, choice was certainly a myth. Even where pupils had done well at GCSE level, they could not necessarily make a choice of A-Level subjects unfettered by policy changes, timetable limitations and school reorganisations. In a number of cases these limitations adversely affected their choice of future career.

Frustrated participation

The picture of differentiation and polarization (Woods 1990) which, as discussed earlier, has been drawn in some of the literature examining the school experiences of working class, ethnic minority or female pupils does not seem to be reflected in the stories of participants in this study. They certainly seemed to have experienced differentiation, by virtue of their family origin, race, class and gender. They also have been excluded from opportunities by limitations placed on their curriculum and career choices. However, their reaction to differentiation does not seem to have been polarization. They did not relate anti-school feelings;

they appear to have been quite keen to achieve educationally and to find themselves rewarding and satisfying jobs.

Brown's (1987) study of working class children in a Welsh town identified a similar type of orientation towards school among his participants, that of 'ordinary kids', instrumentally oriented towards school and future career prospects, but unable to fulfil their hopes because of structural inequalities, institutional barriers and pupils' internalisation of restricted educational and employment prospects Like some of the 'ordinary kids' described in Brown's study, the participants in this study were keen to get on well at school, worked towards qualifications and did not find themselves in open conflict with the school ethos. Rather, they were frustrated by the barriers of lack of interest, guidance and support which were placed in their way, and over which they had little control. As will be apparent in the following chapter, this sense of thwarted aspiration was also experienced in the advice they received from careers officers and in the nature of the vocational training to which they were frequently directed.

3

POST-SCHOOL PROSPECTS: FRUSTRATED PROGRESS

It's just like you're blindfolded; you can't see the path ahead.
Maureen: REACHOUT participant

I think they looked at my school report and said: Well, we haven't got anything for you; you are not suitable for anything, and you're not going to go anywhere. That was her attitude.
Pauline: REACHOUT participant

As participants progressed through school they inevitably began to consider their future career options: whether to stay on at school to study for A-Levels, whether to undertake a vocational course, or whether to leave school and look for work straight away. I explored with them how they viewed the careers advice and guidance they had received towards the end of their schooling. If family members were unable to offer careers advice and support, the role of the official careers guidance service would be crucial in helping to shape aspirations. I therefore asked them about the quality and frequency of any careers guidance they received and how this had influenced their career paths. I also asked what education and training they had undertaken in the years between leaving school and becoming involved with Reachout.

What their stories reveal is a sense of hopes unfulfilled and aspirations undernourished as students attempted to build their careers and ensure their own and their children's futures. Far from compensating for lack of family knowledge, official sources of guidance appeared to compound existing disadvantage. Careers advice seemed to have been perfunctory and, in some cases damaging to their sense of themselves and their ideas for the future. Furthermore, post-school education often involved them in a variety of forms of vocational education and training which seemed to lead them down a cul-de-sac of poorly paid work with few prospects for career advancement.

POST-SCHOOL PROSPECTS – OFFICIAL ADVICE, SUPPORT AND GUIDANCE
Oh no, it's not for you: Joy's story

Joy felt that her parents did not have the experience of the education system to help her identify a career direction.

> What I would have liked – my mum and dad giving me more incentive, more support. I think they themselves, coming from the Caribbean, weren't aware of the system and how it worked, and where they can help. So I think that's where they failed in that sense.

She remembered a careers advice session, just before she left school:

> If I had an idea, I felt that the career advisor would say to me: Oh no, you're not suited for that, try this. It wasn't a matter of listening to me, and helping me to find out exactly what I wanted. For some reason, if I said nursing, they said: Oh no, it's not for you, sort of thing. On the other hand, if I had said I'd thought of counselling, they probably would have said: No, not counselling, go into nursing. I think that they have this stereotype, ideology of thinking that Caribbean people would be best off nursing, singing or dancing, running and so forth. Anything else outside that, it was: Oh no, it's not for you. So I didn't feel that I got the best information and support from the careers advisor.

The birth of her first child gave her an interest in childcare work. She became a volunteer in her daughter's nursery, and was encouraged to train as a nursery worker:

> I got the information and I went to [Eastland] college to do my BTEC in Nursery Nursing. It was a struggle – having a baby; travelling

there as well, and having no sort of income. But I did it. I enjoyed it. And again, I think I got stuck there, not knowing where to go after being qualified.

Joy obtained a job as a home-school liaison worker. It was a short term funded post:

> It was brilliant. I felt that I was in control. Talking to parents, solving parents' problems.

Joy did a counselling course. However, her work contract ran out. Eventually, she got a job as a classroom assistant:

> I don't enjoy it because I'm not stretched. My brain is not going any-where and I just feel it's time for me to move on.

She undertook a number of courses, in an attempt improve her employ-ment position:

> I've got my BTEC in nursery nursing, I've done two levels of counselling. I've done so much; I've done my first aid; I've done that introduction to social care. I was covering ground I'd done already. These little courses – basically they're not worth much. They're moving me no further.

She undertook a part-time certificate of higher education in Psychology. After two years of study, she was still in the same, unsatisfying job, still unable to move forward.

Bits of courses: Patricia's story

Patricia was keen on pursuing a career in social work when she was still at school:

> I knew I wanted to do some sort of social work. I didn't know much about all the different types of social work you can go into then.

However, her careers advice did not really help her to plot a path to her goal:

> We had a careers lesson every week. It was the class as a whole, that's how it was done. And every now and then you had to go to the careers office, outside of school. I think that they were showing you the jobs that were available.

Patricia managed to find a course which interested her and went to further education college after leaving school with GCSEs:

> I went to [Marton] College, did a social care course, which I didn't complete, because I had a child. I did bits of courses here, bits of courses there. I did a secretarial course and then I did another access course for two years. But I knew I had to work to support the family. So I slipped into that for a while – caring work, residential and community care.

Patricia was torn between her need to earn money to look after her children in the short term and her desire for a career which she saw as worthwhile:

> When I had a child, it just threw me out; all my circumstances changed then. I wasn't sure what I was doing. I had to put things on hold really. It was the need to earn money. When I went through the course, I was working as well. Work took over and I put more hours into the work; that's what happened.

As an unqualified care worker, her prospects were limited. By this time, Patricia had three children. Another was on the way:

> The reason why I decided to go back and do social work [was that] the only jobs that I could get were just – the more manual side of it. And I wasn't earning that much money to make a difference, so I thought I might as well go back and get what I really needed . . . I could have put it off for ever. It got to the stage where it wasn't worth working in the kinds of jobs I got. I wasn't going to earn enough. So I thought: I'm pregnant now, I might as well take this opportunity, because I'm going to be out of work for a bit. When I've actually had the baby, I'm not going to be able to afford to go back to work and pay childminder's fees. I might as well use this opportunity to get the qualifications out of the way while the baby's young.

Patricia started studying with REACHOUT. She began her social work training at university the following year.

I've always wanted to have a career: Helen's story

Helen felt unable to progress at school, because of her sense of marginalisation as a black pupil in a mainly white school. She felt discouraged by her careers advisor:

> She pushed us into doing what we didn't want to do. Was it teaching? Was it the thing that everyone wanted to be – an air stewardess? I think I wanted that as well. The glamorous life. And she said: No, I think it's best you go and do something like cooking. And I did get a job in catering. I left about two months afterwards, I hated it so much. And then you thought, what else can you do? So you hop from job to job until you meet some sort of man, and then you fall in love, type of thing. Then that's the end of that.

She described herself as doing nothing educationally for about fifteen years. She began a vocational qualification, but did not complete it:

> Because I came up against opposition all the time, I just thought, why bother? My other friends they fought through, but I just thought – oh I can't be bothered.

At this point, Helen became pregnant with the third of her four children. She gave up her course, and did not think of returning to education until her fourth and last child was born:

> Well, I got divorced. Then I realised I was on my own. My mum died and I thought, I'm on my own. I can't go to anyone and say: Can I have some money? And I didn't have any savings or anything. And I thought, I'm going to have to try something because I know I've got to look after my family. And I thought, well I like people. What can I do that will involve people? So I thought well, social work seems something that I could try. And I was sitting in the school one day, and somebody said why don't I try REACHOUT?

By chance, she met the wife of the local vicar at her child's playgroup:

> She said: Why don't you try REACHOUT, because I was saying I'd like to try social work . . . And I sat and thought about it, and I thought: that sounds good. And she just said: Try it. She was saying about higher education. And I thought: Ooh I haven't really done anything in the last few years, so that might be a problem. And then I thought: Yes, I'm going to try it, because you don't know until you try. So I tried it, and then I came on the phone. Do you remember?

Official advice, support and guidance

However well motivated, the participants in this study appeared to be disadvantaged in terms of advice and support from outside the family, as well as from inside. Helen, Joy and Patricia all described being channelled by their school and career advisors into poorly paid work, with few prospects, and which acted merely as a bridge between school and child-bearing. They lacked the social and cultural capital (Bourdieu 1997) which may enable middle class white students and their parents to plot career paths on a long term basis.

Informational disadvantages seemed to be compounded by the way in which careers advice was offered, particularly to those who, by the age of sixteen, had not been considered successful at school. From their point of view, the careers advice they were offered was short-term, negative and based on their existing qualifications, rather than on their aspirations. There were indications too, from their descriptions, that careers advice tended to be based upon gender and ethnic stereotypes. It did not appear to take into account factors such as enforced school absence, home difficulties or other problems with school and learning.

It seemed that, at an early stage, participants were screened out of further academic opportunities because of assumptions made about their perceived failure, rather than an assessment of their future potential. If they did decide to continue in education or training, they tended to be directed, by teachers and careers advisors, towards vocational courses – secretarial work, nursery nursing and catering for the women; engineering, carpentry or draughtsmanship for the men. The option of re-sitting GCSEs, or staying on at school to improve existing qualifications and raise their academic profile seemed rarely to be offered.

McDonough (1995) has highlighted the role of the United States' educational guidance service in determining and perpetuating educational inequalities. She stressed the importance of school and family in affecting individual pupil outcomes and drew attention to the role of guidance services in influencing the choices of pupils in accordance with their class position. A similar phenomenon seemed to be at work in the role of the careers service in demarcating the future career and educational options of the participants in this study.

Careers guidance seemed to operate, not as a mechanism for enabling them to explore their options and broaden their choices, but more as a means of closing options down, consigning participants to roles, according to their gender, race and class. It fitted them for vacancies available in the short term, thereby reproducing educational, occupational and economic disadvantage (Lynch 1989, Morrow and Torres 1998). The result was that participants later found themselves trapped in unsatisfying, insecure or poorly paid work and unable to see a way out of their situation. Laura's story illustrates some of the effects of this closing down of options.

The middle class school student who successfully takes the requisite number of GCSEs, stays on to the sixth form and takes A-Levels, and applies for and gains a university place at the age of eighteen or nineteen, has the benefit of advice and guidance at each stage in the process. At university, other opportunities open up. Peers and tutors, operating in the university milieu, provide a sounding-board for the student to consider her future direction. Counselling and advisory services are on hand, and a network of colleagues develops. Outside school or university, the middle class student may also have access to informal support, advice and guidance from family and friends, experienced in the ways of higher education. Parents may know what questions to ask teachers and careers advisors and may be, as Reay (1998) has suggested, more confident in approaching them. Thus the working class and ethnic minority students in this study seem to be doubly disadvantaged by their lack of access to either formal and informal sources of information, advice and guidance.

POST-SCHOOL PROSPECTS – VOCATIONAL CUL-DE-SACS
The job I want to do is out there: Laura's story

Unsure what she wanted to do after leaving school, Laura was directed towards a Youth Training Scheme in catering by her careers advisor:

> I didn't have a clue what I wanted to do. So I ended up doing a YTS in catering. I think I was into cooking because I had to cook at home for everybody. So I think that started it off. Then I left that and went into retail. I stayed there until I had my daughter.

After having her first child, Laura stayed at home for ten months to care for her and then decided to do a childcare course:

> I thought, well this is what I want to do. I want to work with kids. I enjoy it.

However, she had another child quite soon after starting the course. She decided to combine caring for her baby son with studying. It was not easy:

> I was going to bed, you know, at about ten o'clock; getting up doing assignments until four or five in the morning; going back to bed; getting up at seven, getting them both sorted and getting the baby to the childminder. It was killing me until he [Laura's former partner] gave up work and stayed home to look after the little one. So in a sense it was easier. But in a sense I was still coming home and cooking, washing and cleaning. And it was: I've been looking after the little one all day; he's been crying for his mum all day.

Laura managed to finish the course successfully but could not find a job:

> I was just exhausted. I had a year's ironing to do! I think I was just utterly tired, knackered with doing it. And then I was applying for different jobs and not getting anything.

After being without work for some time, Laura started a number of different courses, including a social science course and an adult teaching certificate. She completed her adult teaching certificate successfully. She found temporary childcare work, but it was poorly paid and offered no prospect of career advancement. Laura wanted to go into school teaching but her childcare qualification and adult teaching certificate were not sufficient to qualify her for entry to school-based teacher training. She needed maths GCSE, which she had not gained at school. She felt stuck in her career:

> The job I want to do is out there, but I'm not qualified to do it. I'm only qualified to be a teachers' assistant. And even that – you go to the interviews – there's so many of us out there.

Laura is still working in childcare.

Vocational cul-de-sacs

Government initiatives, such as that which funded Reachout, tend to operate on an assumption that the residents of the area identified for special help or action are suffering from deficits in their education, skills and training. What became clear during the course of this study was that most of the participants had been educationally or economically active since leaving school, but had been unable to use their training and education fully to gain a more satisfying job, better pay and a better lifestyle for themselves and their children. Their desire to move on educationally was generally prompted by a combination of factors, personal, social and economic.

There were both positive *pulls* towards education, when barriers to learning which had seemed to exist began to be broken down, and more negative *pushes*, when participants realised that their chances of moving on from their current position were limited by their lack of degree level or professional qualifications and that to make career headway they would have to consider a return to education. For a considerable number of the women, it was their childcare and family responsibilities which impelled them towards higher education, but ironically, pregnancy and childcare responsibilities held them back and meant they had to abandon courses they had undertaken.

Pascall and Cox (1993), in their study of women returning to higher education in the late 1970s and early 1980s, cite decreasing childcare demands, marital breakdown, economic and career considerations as the main reasons given for deciding to return to education. They also refer to the complex and interlocking nature of these factors. In the Reachout study there were similarities in reasons given for considering a return to education. However, there were also some differences. Twenty years separated the experiences of these two groups of participants. Patterns of family life have changed considerably over this time; the proportion of single parent households has increased and the divorce rate has continued to rise (Office for National Statistics 2000). The majority of the women in this study were not married. Most were lone parents, taking sole or main financial and caring responsibility for their children. Overwhelmingly, they were in low paid or part-time work, or dependent on social security benefit. They aimed to improve their occupational and financial position through higher education and professional training. The situation seemed to become most urgent for them at the point where their children were still young, rather than when they were becoming less burdened by their childcare responsibilities. They realised that if they did not do something quickly, they and their children would continue to struggle financially.

Over half the participants in this study already held vocational qualifications, in business studies, administration, catering, engineering, nursery nursing or social care. However, it had been difficult for them to use the knowledge and experience they had gained to progress to higher education. There appeared to be few signposts from a vocational course to a higher education opportunity. It seemed that post-16 vocational training qualifications were not recognised as suitable entry qualifications into higher education and professional courses. Without a significant change in direction, there was little possibility of obtaining increased responsibility and pay through promotion: the classroom assistant could not become a teacher, the veterinary assistant could not become a veterinary nurse; the residential or day care worker could not become a social worker.

A particular area of difficulty was in progressing from a nursery nursing qualification (the NNEB) – a career generally regarded to be the preserve of women – to higher education. The NNEB has limited currency as far as higher education entry is concerned. Students who did not have access to well informed advice and support found this a barrier. If they wanted to train for teaching later in life, they would have to go back to study, take A-Levels, as well as a GCSE in Maths and English, often while working full time and bringing up a family. The need to begin studying all over again deterred them from applying to train as a teacher. This was particularly the case for Nargis and Joy, and for Laura – an experienced and trained child care worker – who felt frustrated in low paid work and short term contracts. Participants were caught in a credentials trap, pushed down a narrow vocational path which often involved low paid, gendered employment. Furthermore, they lacked the resources in terms of money, time and information to escape from the trap.

It was often a chance encounter with a source of advice or the opportunity to attend a short course which made these people feel they might be able to return to education – a tendency also noted by Susan Weil (1989). A number of those interviewed were able to identify key people who had encouraged them to move forward or had provided crucial information (Burton 1993). Frequently, this was a complete stranger. Helen was advised by the vicar's wife at her child's church playgroup; Siobhan was told about Access Courses by a woman who interviewed her for a job, who happened to be married to a college lecturer; June gained helpful advice on the Open University from the man who came to collect her benefit book; Joy was much encouraged by the headteacher at her daughter's nursery school; Derek was advised by his physiotherapist; Seima by a health visitor. Direction and support seemed to come in a rather haphazard way, and not from official sources of educational help and guidance. The formal structures of educational and careers advice for adults did not seem to be there to help them make choices when they were ready to do so.

Jim and Paul eventually felt able to move on educationally because earlier problems with dyslexia had been identified and they had found ways of dealing with their reading and writing difficulties. After a school life punctuated by bullying, Maureen found that, as a parent undertaking a parent volunteer course at her children's playgroup, she was treated as an adult and no longer made to feel 'stupid' in relation to education. This gave her the courage to go further, and to feel that she could perhaps achieve educationally. Attendance on short courses of a practical or vocational nature frequently provided the impetus for being able to leave past, unhappy experiences of education behind and look to the future.

An unanticipated aspect of Reachout's intervention was the extent to which it was used by participants to help them to identify their study and career options. As a result, this rapidly became a key aspect of Reachout's work, and was recalled by a number of participants as being crucial in removing informational barriers. Clearly a major difficulty for adults, given the market orientation of much further education provision, is access to advice and guidance which puts their needs at the centre of the picture, rather than colleges, courses, and per capita funding arrangements.

Frustrated careers

In the debate about participation and non-participation in education, the tendency to blame the victim rather than focus on the social and economic determinants of participation has been noted by a number of writers (Woodrow 1999, Gorard *et al* 2000). What was notable about the educational careers of those interviewed was not their previous lack of participation but their high level of commitment to education as a way forward. Reachout did not appear to have attracted non-participants. All but three of those interviewed had taken part in one or more formally organised courses in the three years prior to their contact with Reachout ranging from basic English, parent volunteer courses, Access Courses, and in one case, the first year of a degree. Doors which should have been opened to them remained closed. They were, as highlighted earlier, frustrated participants. They had been active educationally but unable to use the education and skills they had gained to win themselves more satisfying jobs, better pay and a better lifestyle. They were frustrated by lack of guidance and support and a sense that higher education was *not for the likes of them*.

The pattern emerging was of the non-traditional student engaged in a struggle against the failure of those who should have been able to help them to take their difficulties and aspirations seriously. This struggle generally entailed returning to both formal and informal education before eventually finding their way, often by chance, towards their goal. The fact that their early efforts were thwarted says more about the kinds of guidance and support they were offered and the low expectations held of ethnic minority and working class women than it says about their potential to succeed educationally.

With Reachout's support, most participants eventually went on to train successfully for their chosen career or undertake degree level education. However, the wasted time and difficulty spent in gaining qualifications so much later in life affected their economic position and that of their children. They were often living on benefit or working in low paid jobs when, arguably, they could have been considerably better off, had the right help been available earlier on. The decision to return to education later in life brought with it risks of financial difficulty, family disruption and personal isolation. While supporting students through this period, Reachout learned from them about ways in which adults can be helped to make the transition to higher education. The impact of this transition is dealt with in the next chapter.

4

GETTING INTO HIGHER EDUCATION

If you're not white and middle class, you're not accepted.
There's nothing overt, you just sense it.

Salma: Brookvale University student

his chapter explores the choices made by participants, how they anticipated entry into higher education and what they found when they first arrived at university or college. By September 1999, of the 37 people who had agreed to participate in the research study, 25 had moved on to higher education. They were distributed throughout locally-based colleges and universities:

ten studied Open University courses

seven studied full-time for a professional qualification in social or community work

five studied full-time for a degree

three studied part-time for a higher education diploma

As the number of participants entering full and part time higher education grew, it was possible to build a picture of how they experienced university life. I kept in touch with the participants as they moved on to university, discussing with them their reasons for choosing one form of study and one type of institution over another. In the final phase of data collection, ten participants were interviewed individually. They had been in higher education for one year and were asked to reflect on their first impressions, their relationships within their institution, their experience of studying and the impact of higher education on their lives. For most, entry to higher education was anticipated with anxiety and experienced as a shock. There were differences, however, in the experiences of students undertaking different modes of study. These will be explored in this and the following three chapters.

THE TRADITIONAL UNIVERSITY: SALMA'S CHOICE

Salma decided to study on a full-time basis as she was anxious to complete her degree and find employment as quickly as possible. In pursuing her desire to study Social Policy, she had two choices of university: 'Brookvale' a 'traditional' pre-1992 university and 'Lowvale' a former Polytechnic. She opted for Brookvale.

> Had I gone through the whole campus and felt the atmosphere, I think it might have been different. One of the reasons I did go to [Brookvale] University was its reputation. It is one of the most prestigious universities in the country. It has a good reputation as far as employers are concerned, and I think that influenced me a great deal.

Salma's impression of Lowvale was that it was less well resourced:

> I heard things like there weren't enough books to go round – they were overstretched in that way. They had big classes. But I think with hindsight it might have been better for me because there are a lot of mature students there. And a lot of ethnic minorities there. And it's just across from where I live.

After a term at Brookvale, Salma weighed the situation slightly differently than she had when making her application:

> So I think perhaps with hindsight [Brookvale's] got a higher reputation; it's more prestigious. But then [Lowvale] has got other advantages for me. I suppose there's more working class students there.

Salma's first term at Brookvale convinced her that she would not advise others to choose as she had:

> I might be able to help in that respect. I'll know exactly what they'll be going through and I'll be able to advise them in respect of which university not to go to. I think if I'd been in a position to hear

someone tell me, if they were in the position I have come from – from a disadvantaged background – perhaps I would have been more thoughtful of which university I should go to.

Salma concluded that the more traditional universities were not serious about widening participation.

> I don't really think it's overt. Nothing is said. You just have the feeling you don't belong . . . They just want a certain type of person. I mean, it's just my personal opinion. I've got nothing to back it up. I've got no concrete evidence or facts, just my opinion. I think they just want to keep the status quo. And I think they might be taking on a few token mature students, because they can say: Oh we've got a few mature students; we take mature students.

TEACHER TRAINING COLLEGE: GLORIA'S CHOICE

Gloria was hoping to become a primary school teacher when she graduated. Highvale College, a small college of higher education, was her first choice:

> The fact that [Highvale] is a small institution, it's easier to make friends, therefore one feels less isolated after a while. My experience has been that because it's more multicultural it seemed more friendly. I'm really pleased that I went to [Highvale], it was my first choice . . . I've heard that in some institutions there are less ethnic minorities.

She started a degree course studying race and ethnicity, but soon found that the course would not lead her where she wanted. She changed to a degree in childhood studies a few weeks after term began.

> I suddenly became aware while on the course that when I had completed my degree, I could only teach in secondary. I thought about the situation and, having worked for the past seven years with children aged five to twelve, I wanted to stay within this age group. It became clear to me during the class induction. It was during this session that I became aware that the ethnicity course meant that I could not teach primary. During the session, the lecturer asked what people wanted to go into once they had completed the course. And one of the students mentioned that she was aware that this particular course did not cater for primary teaching. For me this was a dilemma. When it was my turn to answer, I just said: I think I'm on the wrong course.

SOCIAL WORK TRAINING: SANDRA'S CHOICE

Sandra's family commitments meant that she needed to study near to home. She received offers of a place from both Lowvale, a large post-1992 university, and Highvale a college of higher education. She chose Highvale because it was small:

> It wasn't as large as the other university, so it gave me confidence. I know I couldn't cope in a bigger environment to start with, after being out of education for so long.

She also knew that she would be with three other former Reachout students, with whom she had shared the experience of applying and preparing for higher education entry:

> . . . I didn't feel that sort of isolation that I would have expected if I didn't have anybody else . . . I had the back-up of other people being there with me, from the project. That just set the scene nicely for myself.

In spite of this, Sandra was still anxious about how she might be treated:

> As far as the fears I had when I went in, hearing about how the institution treated minority groups – What is going to happen? Are they going to be picky with me? But having a few more minority students with myself, it helped.

Choice of mode of study

Participants' choice of how, where and what to study was constrained by their financial and family circumstances as well as by their perceptions of themselves in relation to particular types of institution. A balance had to be struck between predicted long term financial gain and short term loss. Considerations of age, race and class were also involved. In the end, the need to stay in the area for family reasons narrowed down their choices.

The first decision to be made was whether to apply to study full time, part time or by distance learning with the Open University. For most, it was a question of weighing financial loss against time taken. A part-time degree is likely to take six years to achieve; a full-time degree three; a full-time diploma in higher education or part-time certificate of higher education will take two years. For a working parent whose aim is to use study as a route to better earnings and lifestyle, it is a difficult balance. Six years part-time study may be too long to contemplate, particularly as gaining a degree does not necessarily guarantee a job and it might be necessary to undergo further professional training. Part-time study is therefore not always feasible. The older the student, the more ageism in the employment market after graduation has to be considered (Glover and Branine 2001, Gaster 2002). If part-time study is rejected as an option, then the prospective full-time student must plan how she is going to manage financially and practically. She may have to give up full-time work; she may have to consider combining part-time work with study and childcare; she will need to contemplate the additional costs of childcare. Then finally, there is the unknowable risk: that giving up work and studying full time may not result in improved career and life prospects. These and other considerations led participants to make choices based on their personal circumstances and constraints rather than on their preferred mode of study, course or institution.

Sixteen of the twenty-five who entered higher education initially undertook part-time or Open University courses. Six of these sixteen part-time students eventually decided to change from part-time to full-time study. This seems to reflect the growing urgency they were feeling about finishing their studies and moving on; and also the particular difficulties of part-time and distance study which this and other research (for example, Bourgeois *et al* 1999) have identified.

Choice of type of institution
Once participants had decided whether to study full or part time, they had to make a choice of university. For Open University students the decision was straightforward. Part-time distance learning was often the only feasible option, because family and work commitments meant that they would be unable to attend a college-based course in the daytime or evening, as childcare costs would be prohibitive. The local choices available to full-time students were two pre-1992 universities, *Brookvale* and *Central*; a former polytechnic; *Lowvale*; and a small college of higher education, *Highvale*. For part-time students, the range of courses available was quite limited and it was therefore usually a question of choosing between the Open University and Brookvale's School of Continuing Education. However, for full-time students, the issue of where to study involved both practical and personal considerations.

Students' choice of institution was, not surprisingly, heavily influenced by family circumstances. Since the majority of research participants had childcare and home responsibilities, selecting a university outside the immediate area was not an option. For those with complex childcare arrangements, a journey to university which involved more than one bus ride across the city, in addition to arranging to drop off and collect children, was not practical. All the students interviewed had selected their institution of study from those in the immediate locality. This inevitably limited their choice of subject and also the range of courses for which they could be considered.

Only one of the full-time students applied to a pre-1992 university. The remainder applied to, and were accepted by, the local college of higher education. There appeared to be a number of reasons for this. First, the students became aware that they were more likely to be accepted by the college of higher education, which operated a mature entry procedure and seemed sympathetic to students with non-traditional qualifications (possibly because the demand for places was lower than at the pre-1992 university). Entry to both social and community work courses was by written test or interview, rather than a prediction of A-Level or Access Course grades. Second, courses available at the college of higher education were more clearly vocational, leading directly to youth and community work, social work or teaching. Rosalind Edwards (1993), in her study of mature women students in higher education, noted a similar pattern of institution choice: the tendency for mature women with non-standard qualifications to enter institutions which had a less prestigious label – in her case, the former polytechnics. She also noted that women of African-Caribbean or Asian origin were more likely than white women to enter polytechnics. Similarly, Green and Webb (1997) reported that students with non-standard higher education entry qualifications 'positioned themselves as other' in relation to the pre-1992 universities.

There seemed to be a class and race divide in institution choice, at least in the minds of the students in this study, and an internalisation of the message that the traditional university was not meant for people like them. Salma alone deliberately chose to apply to the traditional red-brick university. She had no clear idea of what career she wanted to follow on graduation but she was well aware of the difference in status between pre- and post-1992 universities and felt that she would have a better chance of employment if she graduated from a higher status university.

By choosing a college of higher education rather than a university, some students clearly felt that they would be more comfortable and less conspicuous and isolated. All the full-time students were of African-Caribbean or Asian origin, and when choosing an institution, they consciously considered the likelihood of encountering racism, individual or institutional. Some were afraid that experiences of being marginalised at school might repeat themselves. A number had anecdotal evidence from friends and family about how universities and colleges treated ethnic minority students, and these concerns affected their choice. However, in reality, these students' choices were restricted. Because of the geographical limitations imposed upon them by their family commitments, they generally had no more than two institutions from which to choose their preferred subject. In the end, regardless of their fear about how they would be treated, they usually had to accept whichever course they were offered.

Subject choice

Almost all the participants in this study were sole or main breadwinners. Although their motivations towards education involved personal and academic as well as vocational considerations, their choices of subject reflected their career goals, and their stated desire to escape from the trap of benefits, low status and low pay in which most of them found themselves. All but two expressed a desire to use their studies specifically to improve their career prospects. For some, particularly the full-time students, vocational motives were directly reflected in their choice of course. Nine of them undertook professional training through studying for social or community and youth work qualifications. Of the sixteen undertaking degrees, certificates or diplomas which were not specifically vocational, fourteen said that they were returning to study for career purposes, with six wishing to become teachers.

The subject and career choices of participants were almost exclusively teaching, social work, youth and community work or social science. This partly reflects the primarily social science nature of Reachout's access curriculum. It may also support the structuralist assertion (discussed in Lynch 1999) that working class students tend to be propelled towards areas of study which reflect their current position in society: in lower paid, caring or person centred work. Alternatively, as Edwards (1993, p. 155) has suggested, it may be that these areas of study are more conducive to mature women students' connecting their own experience to their academic lives.

ANTICIPATION
My main worries are just the kids: Helen entering Highvale

Helen gained a place at Highvale College to train as a Social Worker. Before starting her course she was anxious. She had been the only black student in her school classroom and was worried about possibly being marginalised:

> You've been stopped at school because of racism; you don't want to go back to where you have to make a stand and say: Well, I'm just as good as you are. You don't want to go through all that.

As she anticipated higher education, she tried to put to one side her worries about coping academically:

> I'm not going to concentrate on that because, if I do, I won't go . . . When I get there, I'll start worrying. My main worries are: will the children be all right while I'm doing it? You know, will I be able to just – without any interruptions. I'm sitting here trying to do the essays and everything and take notes, and then the kids are in the background going: "Mum!" That worries me more: "Mum! Mum! can I have this Mum?" And I'm working, and I'm thinking, if I put them in bed and get back to it; but you've lost your thought. That is hard. And I'm thinking, if I put them in bed for seven o'clock, and I do this and I do that. I've trained them badly over the years; they don't go to bed for seven o'clock. They won't do it now. Now I have got to get them to somebody's house so that they can take them to school. So I have to get up at seven o'clock, get both of them ready, do you understand? But at least I'll have all day to myself. I'll be at college all day, and I'll have Friday with the ironing, the washing, the shopping. If I had somebody to help me it wouldn't be so bad. But it's everything. That's my main worry. Nothing else. Because I know that will be the problem. I'll still have to feed them; I've still got to make sure they're nutritiously fed. So I can't be saying: Oh they'll have a packet meal every night. That's my main worry, Marion.

Helen was afraid she might not be able to cope, but she did not want to contemplate the possibility as the stakes for her were high:

I'm going to try. I mean, if I try and fail – I don't like the word fail. But I have to try to the best of my ability first, and I intend to. I've got to try every way, every avenue. Then I can say I'm beaten. But there's no beaten. I'm too old to be beaten. What am I going to do? I've got to look for something else and I don't like boring laborious jobs. I can't stand them, Marion. And I need the money to look after the kids . . . I don't want to go backwards; I don't want to be doing some silly job. I want to get up there . . . It will be my new life. Honestly Marion, I really do hope. I'm going to try my hardest. I'm really going to try. Just as long as everything else works for me – the childcare and all that. That's another thing I was worrying about.

Anticipation

Mature students from non-traditional backgrounds may be entering an unknown world when they gain access to higher education. Frequently there is no family experience of university life against which to assess the likely impact of higher education. Apart from attending an interview or, in the case of an Open University student, receiving written information, there may have been little preparatory contact with the university beforehand. The stakes are often high. Intending full-time students may have given up secure full-time jobs. A number of participants had bad memories of their earlier education and were afraid of failure or of past humiliations being repeated.

For full-time women students with children, there were also practical problems to be anticipated and overcome: finding time to study when the children want attention in the evening; arranging for the children to be picked up from school if lectures go on beyond 3 pm; finding and paying for child care. A great deal of preparation was needed, over and above academic preparation. Issues of finding and affording childcare occupied the minds of all the mothers who were about to study full time. For some, it threatened their chances of going to university. It was exacerbated by the fact that help from university access funds could not be applied for until after students had enrolled and applied for their maintenance loan. Because of a funding anomaly, the four social work students taking up places at Highvale College discovered quite late in the application process that there was no access fund to which they could apply. These were problems in which Reachout intervened, helping to find appropriate childcare and raising funds from charitable trusts to pay students' childcare costs. For the students in this study, practical concerns dominated their anticipation of university life. Although they felt a sense of achievement and excitement at entering a new world (Leonard 1994), they were also fearful of the unknown.

FIRST IMPRESSIONS
All the others were young: Hazel entering Highvale

On the first day of her youth and community work course, Hazel had mixed feelings. She was excited but she was conscious of the differences between herself and the other students:

> I was actually quite nervous on the first day. I realised that it was more than I anticipated. Having two small children, finances and time-keeping as well. I often wondered if I had bitten off more than I could chew. I was excited and anxious but really looking forward to my first day.

> Of my full-time bunch, I must have been one of the oldest ones. It wasn't multiculturally mixed. There was only two black females: myself and Marcia and two Asians. All the rest were European white people. So really, although the others were brilliant, I sort of took friends with Marcia who was black and who had children. We sort of related to each other because we had something in common you see.

Her anxiety rose during her first few days at college, but she was determined to carry on:

> When I saw the students, I was really frightened. And the first assignment we had to do was write a bit about ourselves and our personal goals and a bit about [Highvale]. And I wrote that my first thought was: What the hell am I doing here? I could be at home with my children. But I was determined to make a success of my life. So I went on, and bear with it, and got through the first year.

It was real shock: Baljit entering Highvale

Baljit reacted strongly to her first encounter with university life:

> I think, having been out of social situations, it was a real shock. Nothing had prepared me. It was a total shock to the system. Fortunately, I latched on to another mature student and that made

me feel a bit better. But the whole thing – I hate to think, if it was a bigger university. I think I probably would have passed out, it was that bad.

She tried to minimise her sense of difference by buying and wearing European style clothing. However, it did not have the effect she intended:

I felt self-conscious about the way I dressed, more than anything – student uniform – jeans and top . . . I think it was the transition – changing culturally into more western surroundings. Because, it didn't feel me. I think it all merged together. It just made me feel as if I stood out like a sore thumb.

Eventually, Baljit decided that it was easier to revert to her own identity:

I carried on for about a month, and then I just slipped back into my Asian clothes. It wasn't really a practical thing to go and buy clothes and I didn't feel comfortable anyway.

First impressions

Weil (1986, p. 226) has described higher education entry as 'an assault on the identity' of some non-traditional students, an attack on learners' confidence. This appeared to be true for a number of participants in my study. Open University students Monica and Sue were particularly nervous and uncomfortable about attending their monthly tutorials. Sue, Jim and Harminder reduced their fear of attending tutorials and expressing themselves in tutorial sessions by deliberately joining the same Open University tutorial group, where they already knew their tutor through their preparation studies with Reachout. With this exception, however, the Open University students did not attend their tutorials regularly. Although they often gave work, distance and other commitments as the reason, some students took avoidance action because of discomfort in tutorial groups. Their failure to attend tutorials deprived them of the only face-to-face link with their tutors and course colleagues. It might also have contributed to the students' tendency to get behind in their work and their ultimate abandonment of their studies. In the event, six out of the ten Open University students did not complete their first year of study; three more did not complete their second year. Only one continues to work towards an Open University degree. Given the pain and sense of failure involved in withdrawing from a course, this is a matter of considerable concern.

For full-time students, the first day at college or university could be nerve-wracking. These fears were somewhat alleviated if they had opted to go with other Reachout students they had already met. On arrival, some of them wondered whether they had made the right decision. The extent of their discomfort varied from the extreme anxiety of Baljit to the mixture of anxiety and excitement experienced by Hazel. Salma and Hazel both summarised their feelings as 'homesickness'. Bourgeois and colleagues (1999) describe students as having to present the self within the new social situation of the university, in order to adapt to their role as students. However, as they also concede, the assumption tends to be that it is the student, marked out as different by her age, class and ethnicity, who is expected to adapt to the organisation, rather than vice versa.

For black students in mainly white institutions blending in is not an option. One of the issues for black and Asian students was the extent to which their ethnicity marked them out as different. Jenny described Highvale as 'a very white place'. Hazel, at the same college, was very conscious of differences in both age and ethnicity: Sandra's concern with difference was linked to fear of being picked on within the institution. These fears sometimes related to previous negative experiences at school. Previous school experience and impressions from friends and family led participants to expect that university was not a place where black people would get equality of treatment. Their fears of overt racism were generally allayed when they actually enrolled as students, and they did not experience the direct discrimination they expected. However these issues did emerge later in their experiences of classroom interaction. The three participants of Asian origin initially dealt with the aspect of feeling conspicuous in a similar way. Salma, Baljit and Seima all spent money on European style clothing so they would not stand out in the eurocentric culture of the colleges and universities they were entering. With so little money at their disposal, it was a pity they felt compelled to spend it in this way.

Past educational experience and perceptions of higher education as elitist, white and not intended for people like themselves, influenced the feelings of students as they entered full-time higher education. Most of those interviewed had only visited their university or college once before they actually enrolled. Their sense of what it would be like was based on information, rumour and perceptions from people outside the university. The level of anxiety of non-traditional students was therefore higher than it might have been, had they been offered the opportunity to check out their preconceptions before enrolling. Bourgeois *et al* (1999) mention the importance of induction days in breaking down some of the anxieties of university entry for students unused to the culture of the university. The students in this study confirmed that when this was available it was helpful. Most helpful of all, however, particularly for black students, was knowing that they were not going to be isolated and made to feel conspicuous. In a number of cases, this meant making the deliberate decision to go to university with people that they already knew or attending a university where they knew there would be a relatively high proportion of ethnic minority students.

The feeling of being different experienced by participants affected the limited choices they were able to make about where to study. It also meant that they acted to exclude themselves from institutions which they felt would not be welcoming. Those who could, developed coping strategies to minimise their expected isolation, either by sticking with other Reachout students, linking up quickly with other minority ethnic students or, in the case of those of Asian origin, by adopting a European dress code which they thought might make them less conspicuous. Gaining access to higher education did not mean that the institution itself felt accessible. The feeling of homesickness, described by a number of the participants, seemed to be an indication of the sharp distinction between university culture and the life culture of participants in this study.

5

THE FIRST YEAR:
JUGGLING TIME AND MONEY

*I think that more money should go to finance higher education
so people like me have the chance to improve ourselves financially, so that they can get away from the benefit trap they get
themselves in.*

Helen: Social Work student

This and the following chapter are based on discussions with
participants before and during the *Students Speak* conference
and on ten individual interviews conducted with participants at
the end of their first year. At this point, all but one of those interviewed
were still in higher education. Only Monica, an Open University
student, had given up her studies. Three others, Shilpa, Carol and Jenny,
withdrew later on. The remaining six are either still on their courses or
have completed successfully.

Lynch (1999) identifies three areas in which class constraints operate to
impede the progress of working class students: the economic, the educational and the social. In doing so, she provides a useful framework for
exploring the first year experiences of these students. Such categorisa-
tions may mask the interactive nature of the barriers which non-
traditional students face, as well as the dimensions of age, gender and

race which interweave throughout their stories. But by identifying class as a crucial factor in creating the non-traditional students' sense of otherness and seeing financial difficulty as a key factor in creating and increasing their problems, it is possible to move away from seeing the non-traditional student as the problem and to focus instead upon the contradictions inherent in widening participation in a society where structural inequalities persist. This chapter examines two aspects of poverty experienced by participants: financial poverty and time poverty (Edwards 1993). Financial poverty may be the lot of many working class students; time poverty is particularly burdensome for older students who are parents.

It's preparing for the unexpected: Baljit's story

Baljit was a lone parent with a five-year-old daughter. Her family and former partner did not support her. She was prepared for financial hardship but by the end of her first year she had run out of money to see her through the summer vacation and could not claim benefit:

> At the beginning, because you're given the money in a lump sum, you don't know what to expect. And granted, my experiences were somewhat extreme, I think a normal mature student can expect to have to budget. And it's preparing for the unexpected. Because anything can happen. In the second semester, we were given a gigantic reading list with about twenty books on it. Fortunately, we didn't need them all. But there's so much pressure on people – to get this book, get that book. There are ways round it. You can look in the library, you can go to a cheap bookshop – it's knowing where to get them. But the pressure can compel you to put out money straight away. Other things, in relation to my daughter – all of a sudden, you need childcare. I've needed it on a few occasions. It's having to consider whether it's important that you stay on at college that extra half hour, or rush home to pick them up. But at the end of the day, it all digs into your pocket . . . And after losing your benefits and maybe prescriptions and dental care, you find that you're living under what the state recommends that you need to live on.

> Yes, I think it's careful budgeting. It may seem like a lot of money at the time, but it's not. Especially when you are later informed that you can't claim income support in the summer period. so it's planning for a fifty-two week year and not for thirty-two weeks in term time.

In spite of frequent financial crises, Baljit was determined to keep going:

> I know it's the best option for me and I don't want to be reliant on anybody else. I want to be financially independent. Although in my darkest moments I've felt I can't cope, I will never give up my degree. With your financial problems, the stress and running around like a headless chicken, I think it's still all worth it in the end.

A hell of a lot of a mess: Hazel's story

Hazel was studying full-time while caring for three children single handed and working part-time. She discovered too late that her student loan was supposed to last her all through the summer vacation. At the end of her first year, she felt desperate, financially:

> I want to bury my head in the sand and stay there forever. Because no one told me that financially you were going to be in a hell of a lot of a mess. Right now, I work part time. I work two hours a week in the evening. And that's paid monthly . . . and now I'm doing two hours in the day, Monday afternoon and Wednesday afternoon, doing two hours each day. I haven't been paid yet because I've only just started and it's paid monthly. And financially I haven't got any form of income coming in. Nothing at all . . . they don't prepare you for this. I can't even afford to pay my bills, because the only income I have is Child Benefit for my son and my daughter. And that I have to survive on. And my son. He gets Job Seekers Allowance every fort-night, and I have to rely on that.

She thought, mistakenly, that she would be able to get help from the Benefits Agency, and applied to them. They visited and said that she might be eligible but that they would have to locate her children's father so that the Child Support Agency could pursue him:

> And I said: what if you can't find him? [They said:] Well, we take £20 out of your Income Support, but it will not affect your claim for Income Support. I kept phoning them. They said: yes, we're writing to you. And the last phone call was: I'm sorry we've decided you're not entitled to Income Support. But they still want to come out and talk about the Child Support Agency. I told them to take the £20 out of what they're not giving me! They're not giving me any money, so why do they want to come and discuss? Out of what they're not giving me! It was really stupid. And twice they came, and twice I refused to see them . . . They made me believe that they were going

to help me, and it didn't happen . . . It's like throwing salt in the wound. But financially, I'm telling you it is hard . . . So I'm thinking: hurry up September. Let me just get back to my books.

Hazel was also aware that as soon as she got her student loan, the bank would take it all:

A lot of us have fallen into the trap. The bank knows that you're going on to the second year. You are going to get your student loan. So they keep telling you: Yes, we'll top it up . . . But then, when you sit back and think how much you owe them, and work out that when your loan comes they're going to deduct all this from your loan, and you're going to be left with a little bit. You'll probably end up having to borrow, to get them to top up again. So you'll always be in that trap with the bank, unless you can find some money to get yourself out of it. But financially, it is tough. I've never been in debt with the bank or anything. Till I started Uni. – that was it.

The haves and have-nots: Salma's story

By the end of her first term at university, Salma was destitute and extremely confused about her financial situation. She had been led to understand that she could as a single parent continue to claim Income Support whilst studying full-time for a degree. But then she was told that she would be liable for full payment of her fees if she did this.

Well, I have to claim a loan because my tuition fees will have to be paid. The thing is, because I'm a single parent, I'm therefore eligible to claim Income Support. But I still have to get a loan . . . But the thing is, I get my Housing Benefit paid. I don't know how that is going to be affected by the grant. I've talked to Social Security, but they haven't been much help . . . I don't think that many people go to university if they are on Social Security!

At the same time, Salma was being threatened with exclusion from university because she had not paid her fees. She approached her tutor for help:

When I went to talk to my tutor about my grant thing, he said: Oh well, you'd better get that cleared up, because [Brookvale] don't hang around waiting for people to pay their tuition fees. They're going to come after you.

During the Christmas vacation Salma found herself with no money coming in, apart from Child Benefit. She also realised that when the immediate situation was resolved, she would still be disadvantaged in relation to other students – unable to afford books or the increasingly essential computer:

> There is an underclass of people, and one of those is the people without IT knowledge. IT is everywhere now. Everybody's got – well more people have got computer knowledge . . . And there's a gap between the haves and the have-nots.

She remarked on the irony of her personal poverty in relation to the course she was studying – Social Policy.

> I mean, one of the really funny things was, in a seminar debate about poverty, one of the girls was talking about poverty and how people can't afford to buy things. And she said: Well, I wanted these trainers, but my mum made me buy them from Marks & Spencers. Marks & Spencers! Poverty indeed!

However, Salma kept the reality of poverty in her life out of seminar discussions:

> I don't tend to broadcast it around. Because it makes me feel apart from the group, you know what I mean?

Financial hardship

Almost all the participants in the study were either in receipt of benefit at the time of their entry to higher education or else were in relatively low paid work. Only four had a partner who was in employment. Financial hardship affected part-time students indirectly. Most of them did not have to pay fees, either because their fees were waived because they were in receipt of benefit, or because Reachout met the cost. Nonetheless, finance was an issue if they were unemployed or in low paid work. The problem of making ends meet meant that time could not be spent studying, but was used in shift-working, doing overtime or more than one job. It also meant that part-time students could not afford the books or computer equipment that would be the norm for more affluent students. For some, like Monica, education was a luxury. That fact that it became a luxury for her which she found neither enjoyable nor useful called into question its value to the relatively poor student.

For full-time students, lack of money was identified as the most pressing difficulty in their studies. Their financial situation changed drastically when they moved from state benefit to student loan. Frequently, financial entitlements were not established until well into the first term, meaning that they were dogged by uncertainty. In most cases Housing Benefit was reduced as a result of the student loan, and students became unsure about their entitlement to health care benefits when they were no longer eligible for Income Support. All the full-time students found themselves in difficulty with the benefit system. Hazel found herself in 'a hell of a lot of a mess'. A major problem for Jenny, Hazel and Baljit was receiving their student loan in a lump sum at the beginning of the term and trying to make it last for four months. Budgeting became very difficult, especially during vacations. Access funds, available to students in hardship, were often paid very late in the term. Students could not apply for additional assistance until they had enrolled. Sometimes university decisions on the disbursement of hardship funds took several weeks. Consequently, these students lived in a state of budgetary uncertainty, unsure how they were going to make ends meet. The banks were seen as part of the process of increasing students' levels of debt and poverty, and reinforcing their feelings that they could not cope. Banks were keen to offer students fresh loans if they were in financial difficulty. The problem for the students was how they were going to repay the debt.

A single parent, Salma, who was entitled to Income Support without having to pass the availability to work test, realised rather late in her first term that she would have to apply for a student loan in order to get help with her fees. She was strongly opposed to the idea of loans. In the end, she had to go through the process of applying for a loan and, in the interim, was left with no funds at all on which to live. Her benefit was stopped when the Benefits Agency realised that she was eligible for a student loan. At the same time, she was being threatened that she could not continue her course if she did not pay her university fees. Donna had similar problems during the first few weeks of her course. She had to take time off to visit the bank manager and to try to find part-time shift work to make ends meet. In the end, she decided to defer her studies for a year as she had lost so much time in trying to resolve her financial worries.

Until recently, no allowance was made by government for the childcare costs of students who are parents. Those higher education institutions which had childcare facilities charged nursery fees which none of the participants could afford, even if charges were subsidised. They had to search for cheaper community based nurseries and after school facilities. This, in turn, complicated arrangements for dropping off and collecting children, and increased travelling costs. Some students were unable to undertake paid work during the holidays or in the evening, as the cost of childcare cancelled out the financial benefits of working.

The sense of poverty in relation to better off students can in itself be isolating. Going home knowing that there are bills to be paid which cannot be paid, and that the cost of travel to college is eating into money for the family budget can set poorer students apart. It may make them feel that they are responsible for not coping as they should. To date, there has been limited discussion about the effects of the introduction of student loans on recruitment of students from financially disadvantaged backgrounds (Callender and Kemp 2000, Knowles 2000). The evidence presented here confirms that finance is a major barrier and that poverty is a reality for participants. Changes in government financing of higher education had a negative impact on their perceptions of their financial situation. Although none was liable to pay the £1,000 fee introduced in 1999, all the full-time students were concerned about the burden of debt they were incurring through the introduction of student loans and were unwilling to apply for bank loans. Thus, they found themselves living in poverty, worrying about paying the rent and buying food and, in Patricia's case, choosing between buying books and buying shoes for the children.

Although the focus of their concerns around finance was government policy, there were also ways in which they felt that educational institutions were insensitive to their situation. Examples of such insensitivity were highlighted in the large booklists given to students, regardless of cost and without guidance as to the need to buy them. There also seemed to be an implicit assumption on the part of universities that students would have access to personal computers. Purchasing a computer was a major problem for almost all the students in the study.

As Lynch (1999) has pointed out, the effects of poverty and debt on the student are both direct and indirect. Lack of money deprives her of books and equipment and makes it difficult to pay bills, get reliable childcare and seek health care. It also has indirect effects. In compelling the student to seek part-time work on top of full-time study, it also makes her more 'time poor' (Edwards 1993), spreading herself between the demands of study, family and work. In the first year, the student inevitably wonders whether she can cope with all this and be educationally successful as well.

TIME POVERTY
It's a lot of pressure: Seima's story

Seima, a lone mother of two small children, was accepted to study for a degree at Highvale College. Almost immediately she started college, both her children became ill:

> It's not an excuse, but my children – because of their being poorly – was the only reason that I was a bit behind with my work. And I did feel the pressure. It's a lot of pressure. Especially when you've got to do your work and at the same time you've got to start revising for the exam.

Seima's childcare responsibilities put severe constraints on the time she had available for studying and differentiated her from other students:

> Because they haven't got the responsibilities that mature students, those with children, have. Because, like one of my colleagues mentioned: When you're at college, you're a student; but when you're at home, you're a mother, you're a parent. You've got to fulfil those responsibilities as well. It's easier for the single student. It's much easier for them, because they've got all that time to do their work. Parents – mature students who have children, they've got to make their time, arrange their time accordingly.

Generally, Seima felt that the college was quite understanding to students whose children were ill, and that they were prepared to give extensions for assignments if they were needed. However, she worried about asking, as she thought it might affect her overall assessment:

> You have to have a really good reason to get an extension because, at the end of the day, it goes on your record.

Seima described the difficulty of studying whilst also looking after the children – even a study week did not help her, as it was half term and both children were at home:

I've had to work extra hard; I've had to work round the clock to get my work done because of my children. We had an independent learning week. For a whole week, the children would be fine. Towards the end of the week, one of them would get poorly.

Things became even more difficult for Seima when her children's nursery was suddenly closed, throwing all her arrangements into disarray. She led a campaign to keep it open, which was not ultimately successful. She overcame this problem and carried on studying. For Seima, it is a struggle, but one that she has to win:

> Because there is a future in what I'm doing. On benefits there's no future . . . I'm not only thinking about myself. I'm thinking about my children's future as well. And I've got to give an example to them, that to do something in life you have to work really hard.

I have to juggle roles: Gloria's story

Gloria had two children under five when she began her studies at Highvale, the youngest having been born only two months before her first term began. She had to organise her life to a tight timetable:

> Well it's important to me to get an early start, to prepare for the day, as I have to juggle roles, because I'm not just a student, I'm a mother. I have to be able to cater for the children also. That part of my life is important because if I could not fulfil some part of my role as a mother to the children, I don't think it would be worthwhile doing a degree. The children are only toddlers so making a six o'clock start gives me time to do light housework and to make sure my eldest son has time to eat his breakfast properly, as he's a slow eater in the mornings. Organisation on weekday mornings helps me to feel mentally in control. In the past, I've sometimes found it irritating if I'm at college and I know I've got a pile of washing to do when I get home, plus assignments. I'm not saying that I'm super-woman, but I know I need to have a certain amount of control within my environment for me to proceed.

After doing the housework, Gloria then had to take one child to nursery and the other to a childminder:

> I drop the children off first. Last year, when the car had broken down, what I had to do is drop my eldest son off at nursery first, take a U-turn, then take the baby to the childminder and then go straight to college. I mean you can if you have to . . . In the past, I've had

some stares on the bus: they're probably thinking: Where the hell is she going? Two bags, one pushchair and two children.

In order to keep up with her reading, Gloria had to use any opportunity available:

> I try to read whenever I can, once I'm away from the children: on the bus, in the bath, sometimes even when I'm walking down the road, I've got a book in my hand, so that I have the gist before lectures. Maybe not in great detail. There's nothing worse than attending lectures and you don't have a clue what the issue is about, especially if it is on the reading list for that particular day.

No time to read: Hazel's story

Hazel's life as a student involved combining the care of three children, an evening placement, part-time work and studying. She was not easily able to compensate for the hectic nature of home life by studying late at college:

> Where I missed out was by having a family, because my group did a lot of after class reading. When the class finishes, at the end of the day, they will go to the library, and they've got their own little reading group. But unfortunately, I couldn't take advantage of that because I had to get home to my little one.

Inevitably, the pressure of her hectic life made her skimp on her work, and rush assignments:

> I'll be honest with you, I used to put it off. It was like: I'll do it tomorrow. I used to count the days down. If I had to hand it in on Monday, I thought: I'll do it on Friday. And I've actually done some where I've sat up all night till Monday morning to do it . . . My biggest problem in the first year was time management. I find it really difficult to manage my time.

As well as blaming herself, however, Hazel felt that college organisation did not help her to manage her time:

> I don't think it actually takes into account the fact that you are a mature student and have a family. Because some days when your children are off school, although they say you can bring them in, they don't take consideration for that day. And the course finishes late in the evening. Some of them go beyond four o'clock. If you live at a distance, it is really tiresome.

One of Hazel's greatest strengths as a trainee community worker, her ability to work effectively with young people and adults in her own community, caused problems with finding time and space for studying:

> Where I live, my house is like a community centre. So that doesn't pave the way for me to break down my time. I have a lot of young people coming. Having teenage sons as well – their friends. And they all think I'm their mum; and everyone around the area thinks I'm their mum. And all their problems, I'm carrying. I have to put all that aside . . . But it's time. When I get home from Uni, I'm so tired. And not only that, I have gone through a lot of health problems. But my main health problem is my vitamin B12 deficiency. And when I'm due for my injection, I'm tired, I'm really, really tired. And my body's just run down. I think that's when my brain switches off. But I'm getting there. Getting it done.

Time poverty

Whether full time or part time, most participants were combining study, childcare and paid work. Seven of the twelve full-time students were also working part time, and eleven of the thirteen part-time and distance students were in full or part-time paid work. Those who were not also in paid work had childcare commitments which made employment impossible or impractical. An important aspect of time management, therefore, was combining study, paid work, and childcare commitments and imposing a structure on these competing demands.

The picture which emerged was one of women constantly running to keep up with all the demands on their lives, but determined to do so. Jenny tried to combine childcare, full-time study and night working. She suffered a series of minor heart attacks during her second term, which kept her away from work and study. However, she returned to both, managed to catch up with twelve weeks lost study and pass her first year. Gloria, with two children under three years, had to be tremendously well organised. Like the other mothers interviewed, Gloria felt that it was essential to offer 'quality time' to her children when she got home from college. This often meant cramming study into odd moments and snatched opportunities.

Managing such tight timetables meant that students were aware that they could not give to their studies as much time as they would like. Rather, they had to develop strategies for coping with the work and passing the assignments without neglecting their family and financial responsibilities. This inevitably involved skimping, reading only what was absolutely essential to pass the assignment. Other than attending lectures, participants on full-time courses were not able to spend time at their college or university learning informally, researching around their subject or attending tutorials. Gloria and Hazel were both conscious of missing out in this respect and this seemed to add to their sense of isolation.

The students' perspectives on their need to meet the demands of both academic and family life closely mirror the views expressed in Edwards' 1993 study, and she describes their situation as:

> Teetering on a knife's edge with a finely-tuned structure of arrangements that they had constructed for fitting family and education into their lives. (p. 73)

Time management was identified as a major issue in ensuring successful completion of their studies. These students put the onus on themselves to solve the problem of reconciling the demands of work, family responsibility and study. However, what was interpreted as time management seemed to be more of a structural than a personal issue, one linked to poverty itself, and to gendered assumptions about the responsibility of women to be home managers and child carers as well as breadwinners.

Time is money, money is time

Lack of finance and time set non-traditional students apart from their contemporaries and from the norms of a university system geared towards the needs and commitments of 'the 18-year-old bachelor boy student' (Edwards 1993, p. 63). Their preconceptions of university were that they would have to adapt their lives in order to cope with its demands, rather than vice versa. Lynch (1999) has described finance as the key factor in impeding the progress of low income students and this was the case for most of the students involved in this research. Like an increasing number of younger students, they suffered financial hardship as a result of changes in the system of financing students over the past twenty years. The removal of the right to claim benefit during the vacation affects all students. The imposition of a system of student loans, instead of grants, puts all students in the position of accruing unwanted debt.

However, there were two ways in which this group of students, as parents, were additionally disadvantaged. First, their status as parents put them under increased financial pressure as they tried to continue to provide for their children in a situation where their financial circumstances were adversely affected. Second, being parents deprived a number of them of the time and flexibility available to other students to work in the evenings and during vacations to make ends meet. They were both financially poor and time poor. Lacking finance, they could not buy themselves more time by investing in childcare provision; lacking time, they could not accrue additional money to buy books, computers or other objectified cultural capital (Bourdieu 1997). Their educational experiences in their first year of higher education were therefore inevitably shaped by these two factors, which were to a large extent external to the institution. Within academia itself, however, there was another set of obstacles to be overcome. These will be examined in chapter six.

6

THE FIRST YEAR:
LEARNING THE RULES

One will tell you one thing: 'This is what we expect here'. And then the other tells you something else. And I think: why don't you come together and decide what you really want . . . How they want it. It's so confusing.

Sandra: Social Work student

A lot is to do with getting on with the tutors, and knowing what makes them tick, and doing an assignment like that . . . You've got to know who's going to help you and who's not going to help you. And if you're not going to get any help, you need to seek out where you can.

Baljit: Degree student

A part from the practical difficulties of lack of finance and time, participants also had to come to terms with what was, for most of them, an alien environment when they entered higher education. Whether or not they had been studying immediately before entry to higher education, the demands of university life presented a sizeable challenge. Students compared themselves to younger A-Level students and initially felt at a disadvantage. With the exception of Harminder, none of them had A-Level backgrounds. Most had only restarted their studies within the preceding twelve months. At the beginning of their higher education careers, they felt at a disadvantage academically, and the learning curve in the first few months was a steep one.

Interviews with ten students who looked back on their first year in higher education provided some interesting insights into the problems of returning to study and how these are affected by the kind of support offered by lecturers and tutors. The difficulties experienced by both full and part time students included time management, reading, and structuring and planning assignments. These in themselves are common enough problems. However, running through these accounts of study issues were the difficulties of understanding what tutors wanted and what advice and support they were prepared to offer, and making sense of academic culture and conventions. The students tended to blame themselves for their inability to cope with the time demands of reading and with understanding what tutors required of them. Thus, lack of time was interpreted as poor time management, and lack of clarity of expectations as personal failing. They expressed a desire for greater support and guidance, but did not seem to feel that they could ask for more help from tutors, nor did they feel that tutors would offer such help.

Furthermore, the stories which follow suggest that students' own life experiences, including those of poverty and racism, were not thought suitable for discussion in the classroom. The reasons given for this were either because it would mark them out as different from their colleagues, or else because such discussion seemed unwelcome among middle class white students. This seemed to be the case not only on degree courses but also on professional training courses, such as social work and youth and community work courses, where anti-oppressive practice was stressed as an essential aspect of the students' expected learning. They reported instances where discussions, particularly about racism, were stifled by the tactics of white course colleagues who would either refuse to participate, or deny the validity of the black students' experiences.

Thus, valuable life experience which these students could have brought to their studies was censored, either by they themselves because they feared being seen as difficult or inadequate, or by other students who were unwilling to explore perspectives other than their own. Thus, the onus was on them to adapt to the institution and its rules, rather than for the institution and its main players to adapt to the fresh perspectives which the students in the study brought with them. Gradually, most began to develop strategies for survival, seeking outside support and learning how the unwritten rules of academic assessment worked. Some, at the end of the first year, could see ways in which their personal perspectives were changing and their self-esteem was increasing as they began to see the real possibility of their inclusion. This sense of personal growth was often at odds with their continued feelings of academic inadequacy.

NOT A READER IN THAT WAY: JENNY'S FIRST YEAR

When Jenny began her full-time studies in community and youth work, she found that her main problem was providing evidence that she was doing the required reading:

> I like to read things I choose to read. And when somebody gives me a book and tells me to read it and then write about it, it's just not going to happen. I don't think I'll ever be a reader. I'm not a reader in that way.

She developed a strategy which she felt would convince her tutors that she was reading:

> If 25 per cent of your marks is from reading, you've got to try and show that, even if you haven't read. I'm not going to sit there and read a chapter, and I'm certainly not going to read a book. But I'll read little paragraphs that I think are relevant to what I'm writing, and it's got me through, and my marks have been fine. But I can't read. If I read too much, it goes over my head. If I'm writing something, I know what I want to say and I need something to back me up . . . then I will find something in a book which goes with that. I'm not going to try to take in the whole book just for one little bit. I have my book next to me and then I can pick out the bits.

Jenny was aware that she needed to offer some evidence of theoretical, as well as practical understanding. Again, she took a pragmatic approach:

> I think you need quite a few theories. If you just work off one, then you probably never get it. If you've got a variety of theories, you'll be fine. But I suppose that comes down to reading again, or just knowing a little bit about certain theories. You've got to have some theories because that's what they're looking for, aren't they?

I don't think the linking of theory to practice is that useful because, I mean, theory is fine, but when you get out there in the field – it's good to have some sort of theory. But, if you're constantly focusing on these theories, it affects your practice. Because you can't deal with people on a theoretical basis can you?

However, Jenny was beginning to make links between her practical community work experience and theory through reflecting on her practice:

I think what helped me was analysing what I'd done and then linking it back. If I look at what I've done and why I've done it, the learning comes out of it. Then I'm linking theory to practice.

THE PROPER LANGUAGE: HELEN'S FIRST YEAR

Helen initially felt intimidated by the status which she perceived lecturers as enjoying:

There's many times I used to look at lecturers and they're very educated and 'up there'.

She found that they were more 'human' than she had expected. However, she had difficulty meeting the expectations of the course, and felt that she had problems with reading and understanding what was required of her:

The hardship was not understanding. When they give you an assignment and say it was on this handout. But my difficulty is not understanding what to do at first.

Helen tended to blame herself for her inability to understand what was required:

I think that there's a lack of my reading ability, which I can't blame anyone for. I can only blame myself because I don't like reading. And if you don't read, you're not going to learn certain things. So I suppose that's to do with me.

Helen also found difficulty incorporating the work of others into her own writing:

It's reading as well as putting what you read into your essay. You can read it and understand. I can read and understand it, but then you have to incorporate it into your own words. But in the words they want you to say it in, not just: She said this, and this is the way it should be. The words, the proper language.

Having been brought up in Jamaica she was aware of dialect differences between her own writing style and accepted academic style. She blamed herself, rather than the limitations placed on her by academic conventions:

> Maybe it's because I have difficulty pronouncing certain words. I avoid using them as they're not familiar to me. When I'm writing I find that because I'm not familiar with those words, it's hard to write them.

Helen was afraid that if she mentioned the problems she was experiencing, it would jeopardise her chances of staying on the course:

> I haven't really gone into it, because I don't want them to say, well, you're not supposed to be on this course, or anything like that. I've come too far now for them to say that, so I don't like raising the issue

THEY JUST GIVE YOU BOOKS: HAZEL'S FIRST YEAR

Finding time to read was the biggest problem for Hazel as she studied for a youth and community work qualification.

> They just give you books; you have to read books. I found that my biggest problem.

Hazel developed strategies for coping with her chronic shortage of time. One was to rely on her own experience rather than her reading:

> And my tutor said to me at the end of my first year that she doesn't know how I managed to pass all my assignments without reading . . . They actually recognised that I wasn't doing a lot of reading. I still passed my assignments, but she wants to know how I did it. I thought – well, maybe experience. I just wrote from experience.

She found practical placement work, group tasks and class presentations enjoyable compared with her difficulty with reading and writing, and gained excellent grades for these areas of her studies. However, class discussions around racism and oppression were often problematic:

> The tutor said, you will never understand how a black person feels about racism. And the other [white] student she started crying, because she didn't think the tutor should say that. It was a really horrible, really funny sort of situation, but it was all swept under the carpet. And I said to the students in the group that it's best we talk about it because it's no good going away feeling that we [the black

students] were against you or anything; but she wouldn't. Everything is swept under the carpet . . . You feel that as a black person
that you cannot bring that up; you cannot bring up whatever you
face as a black person, because the other students – the non-black
students, they feel that you are just looking for attention and that
they face racism as well. And that's all they come up with: 'We face
it as well'.

Hazel was anticipating year two and the difficulties ahead, but knew she
had to keep going:

What keeps me going – I don't want to live on Income Support for
the rest of my life. I want to be able to better myself. I'm doing this
for me and my children . . . So I'm going to continue, if it means I'm
going to have to suffer I'll do it . . . I know it's going to be hard, and
I'm going to have to work on my time management. That's my
biggest problem.

Being readers

Reading academic texts was not an ingrained habit for most of these
students and required a great deal of effort. Skills of reading selectively,
using a book's index to find relevant information, reading for understanding, rather than to find quotes which can be lifted wholesale and
put into assignments, were not highly developed. Not being readers *in
that way* – the academic way – was a problem and was indicative of the
distance which they felt between themselves and the expectations of
academic life. They tended to see their lack of academic reading skills
as a personal failing or a time management issue they would need to
rectify if they were going to succeed.

These difficulties may well be experienced by many students new to
university, whatever their backgrounds. However, the disinclination to
read was exacerbated by their difficulties in finding the time to do it.
This was hardly surprising, given the complexities of their lives as
parents and workers. These students could not go to the library and find
a quiet place to read; like Gloria, they had to snatch time to read at bus
stops, in the bath, or when the children were in bed. Reading had a relatively low priority, and was more of an emergency activity undertaken
when an assignment had to be handed in.

On courses of professional training it was possible, to some extent, for
them to rely on their life and practical placement experience, and to

relegate the importance of reading. Jenny developed her own strategy for convincing her tutors that she was incorporating her reading with her practical experience on placement, and Hazel relied heavily on her experience in the community prior to coming on the course. The students' problems with reading were confirmed by feedback from their tutors, which indicated that they did not show sufficient evidence of reading in their assignments. Lack of time, however well managed, was an issue in being able to live up to the university's expectations. Sometimes it meant reading in a highly instrumental way to convince the institution that its demands had been fulfilled.

WHAT DO YOU WANT? SANDRA'S FIRST YEAR

Sandra found planning and writing assignments particularly difficult:

> Planning assignments is my worst, it's my weakness definitely. I can say what I want to put in it, but it's how do I do it? What comes top, second, third? I know I can write. It's just that initial help to say that should go first, second or whatever. Once I've got that, I can do an assignment.

There were inconsistencies between tutors in the guidance they were prepared to offer:

> Some give you guidelines, and some don't. It's like, how do you want us to write this? How do you want us to do it? I would go out and know how to work practically. But writing, it's like – what do you want? . . . It's getting it structured the way that it suits them and suits their needs.

For Sandra, in a minority among a majority of white students, there were other problems:

> When it came to black perspectives, race and all that: black issues, there was always a problem. You'd find the white group would say: Why do we need to learn this? In everyday situations on the course, from day one to the end, we've got to learn as blacks, to cope. Why shouldn't you have an understanding of the issues too? . . . We had two black perspectives lessons, over a year. I was thinking there should have been more. I think these courses are necessary, because they're not just working with one group of people, they're working with different minority groups.

> We're not saying you're racist, we're saying racism is prejudice and power. We're saying, whites seem to have that power, because

they're in a majority. But it's always: you're getting at us, you're saying we are racist. We're saying: No we're not. But we have to say
how we feel.

You could feel the tension and you'd think: Now, are we going to
say anything? You know, just in case they use it against you. You
need to say something, but you can't. You need to address yourself
to it and you can't do that.

It's about evaluating your personal values. What are your motives?
. . . Obviously, we all have our own beliefs and values, but it's about
acknowledging those. And it's about oppression at the end of the
day.

Sandra passed her first year and was anticipating her final year:

I just want it to be over and done with. I've got through the first year;
I've survived. I have got to times of thinking, I don't want to do this,
but then all I can see is that light at the end of the tunnel.

Writing: what do they want?

Linked to the issue of reading was that of incorporating what has been
read into a reasonably well structured written assignment, and balanc-
ing personal experience with evidence of reading. On courses of professional training, linking theory to practice was also a difficulty. After
a year, these students had developed an awareness of the need to
plan and structure essays, but were still uncertain about whether they
were getting it right. They found it difficult to understand what tutors
expected. *What do tutors want?* was as a problem in structuring essays,
coupled with an apparent communication difficulty between tutor and
student about giving and getting guidance. From the students' point of
view, tutors seemed unwilling to give specific guidance on the assignments they set. Some, like Helen, were reluctant to ask for help, for fear
of being thought inadequate. Others, like Baljit, quickly learned that
tutors varied in their willingness to offer help and support, as well as in
their expectations of student assignments.

Of the ten women interviewed at the end of their first year, seven regularly sought Reachout's help with their studies. Sandra, Helen and
Jenny felt that outside help was essential, since guidance was not forthcoming at the university. This raises the question of what students do
when there is no outside help to be found. Few of the participants in this

study had family members who had been to university. The support of friends and family which might be available for middle class students, was not there for them. The peer group support that younger, more campus based students could rely upon, in the library or the common room, was not available to older students with family commitments. Our student group generally went straight from lectures to home responsibilities. Bourgeois *et al* (1999) see the problems experienced by new students in handing in their first essays as being relatively easily overcome, once they learn to approach tutors. For our student group, the difficulties were more sustained. They found themselves working in the dark, seeking outside help and trying to find out what individual tutors expected.

IN SOCIAL POLICY THEY TALK ABOUT PEOPLE LIKE ME: SALMA'S FIRST YEAR

When she started university, Salma was shocked at the lack of support from tutors, and their apparent lack of interest in students' concerns:

> I don't think they're very helpful at all really. I think that they think you're there, you should do your work and get on with it.

> They're here just to give lectures, talk about things they're interested in, and that's it. There's no back up, no support.

> I mean, the lectures are fine. You might have the odd lecture where he goes through the material really fast, but that doesn't happen very often. It's not difficult to grasp what they're talking about.

Although she was able to cope relatively well academically, Salma felt deprived materially in relation to other students. She lacked some of the material goods that better off students were able to take for granted:

> I think study-wise, it's been fine, but emotionally, it hasn't. And in some respects – with computer knowledge, or in my case a lack of it – it has been very depressing for me . . . I've felt left out because I've got no knowledge. And in fact, I've got no computer at home. All the other students I've talked to have got a computer at home. Even the mature students . . . It's made me feel more disadvantaged than I was already feeling.

Salma could see the contrast between the content of her studies in Social Policy, poverty, disadvantage and discrimination, and the reality of her daily life, which she was unable to communicate on the course:

> Well, they talk about people like me in Social Policy, with disadvantage. And I feel as if I'm living Social Policy, rather than just reading it from the textbooks, which other students are.

She keenly felt her multiple disadvantage:

> I mean, I know I'm not alone, but the thing is, I feel more disadvantaged because, you know, they talk about ethnic minorities and how they are discriminated, and they talk about single parents, then they talk about women. And I'm in all those groups.

There was, for Salma, a gap between the academic study of poverty and any acknowledgement that it might actually be a daily reality for some students.

I JUST FELT A BIT OUT OF PLACE REALLY: MONICA'S FIRST YEAR

Monica, a lone mother of two children, with a full-time job, was enthusiastic about starting with the Open University:

> When I first started, I was very enthusiastic. I read all the books and I thought: yes. I pinned up the timetable and I thought: I'm going to do this.

However, her plans went awry almost immediately, when she missed the first Open University television programme, which delayed her handing in her first assignment. From then on, she was unable to catch up:

> I'm not sure what happened. I missed the TV programme, and once I missed the first one, I seemed to slide, because there was nobody there to tell me that there's a TV programme, or there's a radio programme coming on. Although I had a timetable, I had all sorts of things going on, and I didn't look at it. And I missed the TV programme. And because of that I thought: Oh God, I can't do this essay, this assignment. It was in fact a week or so late.

Monica's optimism about Open University study dissipated rapidly. Her first tutorial gave her a sense of being out of place. Other group members did not seem to have the same background or constraints as she:

> Unfortunately, I was with people who did everything on time and didn't seem to have problems. They mainly lived on their own, or they went to work and did their assignments when they got home. When I went to the first tutorial, they were even giving in their

essays two weeks before it was due. And I was saying, I haven't started yet. That sort of thing. And they would just look: Oh why? I did feel a bit uncomfortable.

She soon found herself isolated as the only black woman as numbers attending the tutorial dwindled:

In the beginning, there was a mixture of women, black and white. Towards the end there was about three men and I was the only woman.

I just felt a bit out of place really. They'd done it all. They couldn't understand my life. The tutor did try and turn things around and get me involved, but it was 'men talk'. To me, very male dominated.

Monica left the course, deciding not to do any further study for the time being:

It's put me off. I want a break from studying . . . I won't say I would never go back into it, but I'm having a break now.

Her early high hopes had been dashed.

Relationships within the institution

A key aspect of settling into university life is forming relationships with personal and subject tutors as well as other students. Clearly, personal preferences play a large part in this process, so generalising is unwise. However, in the accounts of the first year students in this study, there was a sense of difference and distance, conveyed through descriptions of the student–tutor relationship. For ethnic minority students, also, there was a sense that their experience as black people was silenced, and they felt alienated from the institution and from other students.

The organisation of tutorial support varied between part and full time students. For part time students, the main point of contact, for both academic and personal issues, was one subject tutor, seen once a week, or once a month, depending on the structure of the course. Generally speaking, no specific time was allowed for part time students to have one to one contact with their tutor. Full-time students, however, usually had a personal tutor as well as different subject tutors and lecturers. The experiences of full and part-time students are therefore separately recorded below. The importance of their fellow students also varied, depending on how much class work was done as a group. For part-time and distance learning students, there was limited opportunity to get to know fellow students, or see them as a potential source of support. Although Reachout was able to offer some community based support to these students, it was not always possible for them to take advantage of this if they also had work commitments.

Part-time students, their tutors and lecturers

Monica and Shilpa, both Open University students, felt they had little rapport with their tutors and received little support from them. There appeared to be a gap of class, race and gender, which made it difficult for them to relate to them. These students expressed reluctance to ask their tutors for help. It is not surprising that Open University students, who are not experienced in independent study and who do not have people around them to help them, find distance study difficult and lacking in structure and support. However, part-time students on courses involving weekly attendance, did not necessarily feel any more supported. Ruth and Joy both successfully undertook a two year part-time certificate in higher education. Ruth felt that as a part-time student, she was 'stapled on to the margins' of higher education, conscious that her lecturer was also part-time and likely to arrive at her evening class after a full day's teaching feeling drained and exhausted.

Whether studying part time or with the Open University, a number of students found the personal and study support they received inadequate. Tutors were seen as being distanced from their students and difficult to approach. The fact that time for individual support was not built in to part-time and distance learning courses meant that students had to make specific approaches to tutors if they wanted help. Lack of confidence and a fear of being exposed as inadequate deterred them from doing this. Like Monica, other part-time and distance learners interviewed thought that tutors did not have time to support them, and would not understand their problems. This had a significant effect on whether they completed their courses. Open University students in particular, such as Monica, felt that it was not worth staying the course.

Full-time students and their personal tutors

Personal tutors were generally not positively viewed as sources of support for the full-time students either. Four of the twelve full-time students in the study were not assigned personal tutors at all. Most were either dissatisfied with their tutors or did not feel that they could approach them for help or support. Gloria did not see her personal tutor at all until her second semester, after she had been away from college because of her child's illness. When she did try to see him, she found that her tutor had been changed and she had not been informed. She did not find her new tutor helpful or accessible either. Jenny felt that her tutor had favourites – and she was not one of them. Returning from a period of serious illness, she went to see her about catching up and finishing her first year. She felt that her tutor was not concerned about whether she continued with her studies or not. The college policy was to provide fortnightly tutorials; Jenny had only three in her first year. Hazel, at the same college as Jenny, was also not convinced that it was worth going to see her tutor. She was not sure it was worth making a special journey to college just to have a tutorial which was likely to be unsatisfactory.

The role of personal tutor can be a difficult one. If the tutor is not also a subject lecturer, there may be limited time for tutor and student to develop a relationship which is worthwhile for the student. It appeared from discussion with the full-time students that they either made little use of their personal tutors or did not get helpful responses when they did. Yet the students expressed a clear need for help and guidance in understanding the academic expectations of the university or college. They also had difficulties with finance, time management and childcare which could have been alleviated by the intervention of a personal tutor. There was a mismatch between students' support needs and what they felt was available to them. This may be due to the increasing emphasis on research within universities, at the expense of pastoral and study support (Jary and Parker 1998). Alternatively, it may be that the needs of non-traditional students are different from those of younger students, with the confidence of A-Level success and the support of their peers (Edwards 1993). Bourgeois and her colleagues (1999), in their study of adult students at Warwick University, report that lecturers said that adult students took up more of their time than the younger ones. Even if this is true, it should perhaps not be regarded as a problem but rather as an opportunity to offer non-traditional students the support they need, without which they feel inadequate and uncertain of their ability to cope.

Full-time students and their subject lecturers

Edwards' (1993) study of mature women students stressed the distance felt by students from their subject tutors and lecturers. With a few exceptions, our students felt that subject lecturers were working to their own agenda, without reference to the needs of their students. Most recognised that there were variations between subject lecturers, and that some were more approachable than others. Baljit, for example, found that lecturers who were closer to her in age were more approachable, and that she was able to share experiences with them. Jenny and Gloria also recognised that it was a question of coming to terms with the different styles and personalities of lecturers. Some would walk in, talk about what interested them and go away again, whereas others would invite participation, show enthusiasm for their subject, and engage students in a good learning experience.

There was relatively little comment on the content of lectures or the academic content of their first year. Few of them discussed what they had learned, except in general terms. Expectations of lecturers tended to be that they came to *do their thing*, and did not have a role in backing up student learning. The variation between lecturers in style, attitude and expectations meant that students had to take what was useful from their lecturers and decide for themselves which of them was most likely to meet their needs.

THEY FEEL WE SHOULDN'T BE HERE: GLORIA'S FIRST YEAR

Gloria combined full-time study for a degree with caring for her two small children. She was one of only two black students in her group and sometimes felt excluded:

> A typical example for me, which has happened quite a few times is during a group discussion. Everyone will get into the groups requested, and there would be a certain two [black students] who are not in a group. But they can see me and my colleague on our own. So obviously you think that they would join the two of us. As far as they're concerned, they'd prefer to link to another group and make it bigger.

Gloria's sense of isolation was exacerbated by the fact that she transferred into the group from another course a few weeks into the first term:

> I used to feel an outsider . . . There are very few ethnic minorities and I think that, as a black student, you become aware of who's on the course and the others become aware of you.

There were other ways in which Gloria felt that the voices of black students were not heard:

> When a black student tried to raise awareness of black issues, then I found the attitude was: What's the fuss? For instance, during a debate about the representation of ethnic minorities in the media, after watching a video about soap powder, the question was raised as to why black people did not feature in adverts in the media. The debate became heated and the impression was that blacks are always making a fuss about nothing.

Gloria felt marginalised because she was a black woman. She also felt that younger students found mature students 'too boring':

> Their attitude is that the older generation are boring. I get the impression that they feel we shouldn't be there. I was talking to one student on a bus; I don't think she realised how old I was. She was saying how she wanted to transfer to another university, preferably where there were more younger students and that it would be more fun. I got this impression off quite a few of the students: that university life is for the under-25s.

Gloria did not feel that she had the support or interest of her tutor either:

> My personal experience of my tutor is that in practice he doesn't always want to find time to listen or offer advice. I went to see him about my placement and his attitude was: I'm busy with assignments for the next couple of weeks. And when I did go back to college to find him a couple of weeks later, I hung around the college for two days and I still couldn't find him.

Relationships with other students: support, isolation and silencing

The extent to which participants were able to draw strength and support from fellow students depended on a number of factors. First, did other people on their course share common bonds of age, status or background? Second, were they personally inclined to use their fellow students for support? Third, to what extent were these other students prepared to work with them and accept their experiences as valid? Of the students interviewed in depth after their first year of study, all had entered an environment in which they were in a minority, either as black or Asian women or as older women, more usually as both. Sandra, Helen, Jacqui and Patricia, going together to the same college to study, were able to draw strength from one another from the first nerve wracking day, and through the trials and tribulations of handing in assignments. Although they were in the minority as black students, they were able to lessen their own anxieties through group solidarity.

Hazel, Baljit, Gloria, Jenny, Monica, Seima and Shilpa did not have the advantage of a ready made group of friends. Hazel stuck closely with one particular student because she was also a black mature student and a parent, and they remained close colleagues throughout their course. After a while, she also found other students on her course co-operative and supportive, sharing notes and helping one another out. Baljit recognised that she was different from the other students in her group and that she did not really have much in common with either the young students who were ethnically mixed, or with the mature students who were mainly white. She would move from group to group in the canteen at lunchtime, talking to all, but closely linked with none. Gloria, at the same college as Baljit but on a different course, felt a more pronounced sense of being an outsider as a black woman. She also felt that younger students found mature students 'too boring'.

The age gap was less problematic on professional courses, such as social work and community and youth work, where most of the students were over twenty-one. However, it was keenly felt by students who were on degree courses where the majority of students were younger. There was a conflict (also noted by Bourgeois et al, 1999, p. 110) between the instrumental orientation of the older students and the more social goals of those who were younger. Younger students were seen as being less serious about their studies, and more likely to abuse the system by seeking extensions to assignment deadlines without good reason, and by exploiting the fact that mature students were given extensions because of personal circumstances, to justify extensions for themselves.

Although most of our group said that they were relieved that they did not experience overt racism, either from tutors or students, there were ways in which their experiences as mature black women were silenced.

Most striking of all, in the accounts of students from three different courses, was the unwillingness of the other students to address issues of racism and difference. This was even the case in courses where a positive orientation towards equality was a required learning outcome, such as the professional training of social and community workers. Hazel recounted an incident (described on page 91) where the mere mention of the issue of racism caused a white student to burst into tears. There was a subsequent refusal to discuss either the specific incident or the issue of racism more generally. Both Sandra and Helen described the silencing of black students when they tried to raise their experiences of racism on their social work course. Helen described how the issue was generally raised at the end of a session, causing it to break up in unresolved acrimony. White students appeared to adopt defensive stances, resulting in a refusal to discuss racism. Sandra and Helen both took the view, which was certainly the ethos of the course, that it was essential to be able to understand black experience in order to be able to work effectively with clients in this field.

Our students felt that lecturers sometimes did attempt to challenge white students' refusal to acknowledge racism, and that they dealt with issues when they arose in the class. However, there seemed to be a reluctance to address racism, a tendency to 'sweep it under the table' and to give the issue too little time. It amounted to a denial and marginalisation of black experience. Despite the accusations of white students that their black colleagues were 'obsessed' with issues of racism, it seems that the black students in this study were remarkably tolerant of being so frequently silenced.

The fact that most of the students in this study did not have much social time to spend at college or university meant that there was not much opportunity to develop supportive or social relationships outside the lecture or seminar room. Where bonds were already developed before the course began, through students' involvement with Reachout, they proved important in sustaining them through difficult times. Where they were not, it was possible for the non-traditional student to feel like a loner or to have only a small group of trusted friends with similar backgrounds. In the classroom itself, it was possible for the majority, particularly white students, to contribute to the marginalisation of minority students, either by physically separating themselves from them, as in Gloria's case, or by rendering discussion of their experiences unacceptable, as in the case of Sandra, Helen and Hazel.

Exclusion in an era of widening participation

There was a sense, in their accounts of their expectations and early experiences of university, that the students in the group were outsiders. They expressed considerable anxiety about what they could expect from university and about the university's expectations of them. Some of their fears were allayed once they arrived at university and found that lecturers were, in Helen's words, 'human'. However, their early fears could have been alleviated if the university had been made more aware of their responsibilities and concerns and had taken steps to bridge the gap between students' lives and the world of academia. Students in the study struggled to manage their personal lives so that they did not jeopardise their studies.

There appeared to be a mismatch between non-traditional students' expressed need for support and their perception of the help they were likely to get from tutors and lecturers. Initially, they felt disadvantaged by the fact that they had not arrived at university via A-Levels. They were not fully conversant with academic norms and conventions. Their difficulties were compounded by lack of time to read and lack of support networks to offer them out of college assistance. Academic life involved trying to understand the demands of the institution, to reproduce its structure and language, and to get by without being revealed as inadequate or unable to cope.

There were ways in which the experience of university isolated and silenced the black and Asian students. Their sense of difference was both emphasised by their conspicuousness in white-dominated institutions and silenced by the failure to value their experience. The experience of this group of mature, black, working class participants was barely acknowledged by the institution or recognised as having potential for enhancing the learning of the group as a whole, and more especially its younger students from white, middle class backgrounds.

Bourgeois *et al* (1999) ask whether universities are acting as a force against social exclusion in this era of widening participation. They conclude, as does the evidence from this study, that this is happening in only a limited way. Looking back on their first year in higher education, Reachout students emphasised the difficulties of coming to terms with the rules and requirements of academia and their constant confusion about what was required for success. However, they continued, for the most part, to express optimism about the rewards which their sacrifices would eventually bring for them and their children. There were however, signs from their descriptions of their first year that there were some personal rewards and achievements too. These are discussed in the following chapter.

7

THE FIRST YEAR:
LEARNING FROM EXPERIENCE

Women often feel alienated in academic settings and experience 'formal' education as either peripheral or irrelevant to their central interests and development.

Belenky *et al* 1986, p. 4

I used to feel really low. I had low self esteem. Going to the post office to cash my Income Support. I used to stand there thinking: what am I doing here? I shouldn't be here. But now, even though it is a struggle financially because of my children and childcare and all that, I still feel proud that at the end of the day, there's going to be a result.

Seima: Childhood Studies Degree Student

Personal change and gains

The picture emerging in the previous two chapters was of a higher education experience far removed from the carefree and intellectually stimulating life portrayed in many university prospectuses. In spite of this, only six of the twenty-five students who entered higher education opted to leave altogether during the four years of the study. Those who left were, in the main, Open University students

107

who had found the isolated nature of Open University study unreward-ing and unmanageable. This picture of disproportionate withdrawal rates among ethnic minority Open University undergraduates reflects the situation within the Open University generally (Open University 1999, 2000). Retention rates of other Reachout participants compared well with national performance indicators for the universities they attended (HEFCE 2000). For full-time students, in particular, once they had embarked on their studies, there seemed to be a determination to complete the course, and a conviction that their efforts would ultimately result in personal and financial gains.

However, from conversations with participants in their first few terms at university, it was not always apparent what they were gaining from the formal curriculum and its teaching. When I interviewed the students as they completed their first year, I was interested in what they felt to be the educational benefits of higher education. I wanted to know how participants saw their experience as learners, and what new knowledge they felt they had gained as a result of their studies.

Some, like Monica and Salma, were unable to focus on learning bene-fits, seeing course content as either irrelevant, or at odds with their own experience. They were preoccupied with the practical and financial problems of being at university. In Salma's case particularly, her sense of isolation and poverty dominated every other aspect of her university experience. Hazel could think of little that she had gained from the aca-demic aspect of her youth and community work course. However, she was preoccupied with the difference between the theory of community and youth work, and its practical application. She felt that what she described as her own moral position and experience were a better guide to action than what she heard in lectures and read in books.

Helen, Baljit, Seima, Jenny and Gloria did discuss the personal gains and changes which they felt had marked their first year in higher educa-tion. However, when talking about their learning, they rarely mentioned the formal curriculum but more often expressed a sense of the wider learning and social benefits of higher education. The gains and changes they described included a broadening of personal horizons, raised self-esteem and a greater sense of social inclusion. The learning which they did describe tended to be connected learning (Belenky *et al* 1986) –

connected to practical experience gained in placement, to their experience as parents, or to aspects of their history and culture. This type of learning was vividly described and contrasted with their earlier descriptions of their struggles with theory, lectures and reading and writing.

I LOOK AT THINGS DIFFERENTLY NOW: LEARNING FOR HELEN

As a student on a Social Work course, Helen saw her learning in terms of a broadened view of the world and a greater sense of personal inclusion and involvement:

> I've learned that there's a lot more going on in this world than I thought. That may not be valid to you, but I've felt that I've been living in a cocoon. And I didn't realise there were so many problems out there that make society dysfunction. And the problems we discuss in class – but when you see the face – when you realise that it's something that you have to deal with. And I've learned another thing about people. I value people anyway, but I value them even more now. Because they're oppressed, they're depressed – they have no choices. What else have I learned? I've learned about society – I don't have the words to describe it – I think I'm more of the society.

Helen stressed the changes in her values and attitudes which had come about as a result of her practical placement experience in the field of mental health rehabilitation:

> I thought all these people were mad, that they were going to attack me . . . but, because at [Holly House], where I was, they were there all the time and you had to deal with them in a working situation, helping them . . . you had to communicate in a certain way . . . I found they were so nice. I see some of them now and they say hallo. Before, I'd be really worried. But now, I know how it all works, and I know that sometimes it's the medication they're on that makes them the way they are. so I understand more about these things. I look at things differently now.

Helen found the idea of linking her practical learning to the theory she was reading and hearing about in class more problematic:

> I find that very difficult . . . It wasn't hard when you sat down and you think: well, that's what they're talking about. If you realise this theory's to do with that. But in your living, you don't think of theories, you just go along. And it's only when they say: well, that's

what you're practising, you realise you were connecting theory to practice.

For Helen, theories were implicit in her action, and made explicit in teaching.

> . . . I think we use theories without knowing them. And when you know the theory you think: oh, this is what I'm using. Oh, I've been using that.

THERE'S A LOT MORE TO EDUCATION THAN WHAT YOU JUST LEARN: LEARNING FOR BALJIT

At the end of the first year of her English degree, Baljit considered her progress and learning:

> It's amazing how much you do learn. You expect a very academic, sort of intense learning. I think it's the continuity of it that makes it cumulative . . . You're not learning a single discipline, you're learning about yourself, you're learning about society, you're learning so many different things. It's only at the end of the year when you look at the pile of notes and you think: do I really know this? When you're applying it to your daily life. Especially with language. Even as I'm speaking, I'm conscious of it. When you've got a chance to catch your breath, I think you'll be amazed how much you actually have learned. And I think my confidence has soared. I think when you tell people you're a student, they automatically give you a certain respect, because they know that you know what you're talking about. You are an intelligent person. You're not trodden on as you would be before . . . You're not seen as an ignorant person. So I think there's a lot more to education than what you actually learn. I think, as a person, it really does build you. And I think it's because it's a goal in my life that I want to attain, it's something that I'm pleased I'm actually dealing with now. And therefore it gives me a certain inner peace. I don't feel second best or ignorant . . . So I think there's a lot more to education that just what you learn. I think only good can come of it. Only positive. With your financial problems, the stress and all the running around like a headless chicken. It's all worth it in the end. I think it's all worth it in the end.

Baljit was also widening her possible career options:

> Like I said, my confidence is growing, so I'm exploring other areas; maybe the media, maybe TV presenting . . . I'm considering law, but I think more likely not. I think I might pursue it as another interest

later on. I might go on to do my PhD. I may very well teach. I may work with children.

Over the course of the year, her confidence had soared:

This might sound a bit – but I've always thought I was meant for better things. But unfortunately the opportunities did not present themselves, or I didn't seize the opportunities. Now's my moment. It's all out there. Go and get it. It's there for Tom, for Dick for Harry – it's there for you.

THE WHOLE YEAR HAS BEEN A LESSON: LEARNING FOR SEIMA

After completing her access course on a part-time basis, studying from home, Seima found full-time study demanding:

It was as if I was getting bogged down, because it was all – something different. And you have to contend with the lectures, presentations and getting to know people and working in groups. I think it was a learning process, you know, a lesson for next time round. The whole year has been a lesson.

Time management was identified as a key difficulty, particularly in view of the fact that she was a lone parent with two children under five:

In three months, you've got so much work to do; so much reading to do. And you've really got to organise your time; and it's really difficult for those people who've got children. And time goes so fast you just won't believe it. You think you can leave it till tomorrow to do it, but when tomorrow comes, you haven't got enough time because there's so many other things you've got to do.

Unlike younger students, Seima had to cope with childhood illnesses as well as her own ill health. Although she felt that the college's policies were sympathetic to mature students with children, she did not feel that her course colleagues understood her situation. When she was absent for two weeks because of illness, they assumed she had left:

They thought I had left because I didn't go in for two weeks. They thought I had left the course. Because a lot of students tend to leave in the first year, don't they? And they thought that I couldn't cope with it or something. And when I turned up again, they were saying: what happened to you; what happened about your assignment? You should have handed it in. I said I had got an extension. And because I got an extension, other students think they can get an extension.

In spite of the difficulties, there were aspects of what she was being taught in her degree in Childhood Studies that had relevance to her own life, particularly as a parent:

> I've learned things I never knew. I'm doing childhood studies and I've learned [things] about children – that I could never have imagined. I mean, childhood never existed a couple of hundred years ago, and I didn't even know that . . . It makes you feel good that you're treating your own children well. It just brings so many things to mind. and it's all a learning process, which I have found stressful, distressing, and at the same time interesting. It's a weird combination.

Broadened horizons

Helen, Baljit and Seima described a broadening of their world view as a result of their experience of higher education. All three had been relatively isolated before they returned to study. Seima had been at home with her two small children, with little contact from her family as a result of her divorce. Baljit had been the sole carer for her four year old daughter, and had experienced years of violence and threats from her former partner, with little support from her family. Helen, too, had been left to cope alone with the two youngest of her four children after her husband had left her. Shortly afterwards her mother had died .

Helen described herself as having lived in a 'cocoon' before she went to university. Through her social work placement she had worked with a group of people with mental health problems. It had caused her to rethink her long-held prejudices and stereotypes about mental illness. Baljit saw herself as entering 'social institutions' for the first time since her schooldays. She also regarded herself as making a transition to 'western cultural surroundings'. At the end of the first year, she had begun to redefine herself and to see a wider range of choices which would be open to her as a graduate. She had started university assuming that gaining a degree would lead her to a career in teaching. At the end of her first year she was considering journalism, broadcasting, drama or the law. Seima was also reconsidering her earlier assumption that she would train as a teacher. Her experience of fighting the closure of her children's nursery and of contributing to the *Students Speak* conference had given her an interest in community-based work with families. Pascall and Cox (1993) and Merrill (1999) noted similar changes in the horizons of their research participants. As they came into contact with a wider range of people, possible career options opened up which they never anticipated. Their attitudes changed; they saw themselves as more open minded and less self-centred than before. At the same time, their self-confidence increased.

Self-esteem

The stigma of dependence on state benefit and the internalisation of media stereotypes of single parents weighed heavily with Hazel, Helen, Salma, Seima and Baljit. They all set their ambitions for higher education in the context of escaping the benefit trap. They were all lone mothers who were unable to undertake paid work because their income would be swallowed up in paying for childcare. These women, who felt they had been labelled as scroungers, could now look the world in the eye and feel a part of it. Even though they remained on low income, and struggled to survive financially, they were conscious of their improved social status. Baljit and Seima both said that they felt that they should never have ended up in the position of claimants, solely dependent on benefit. Their strong desire for inclusion was in contrast to the sense of exclusion which they had felt as lone parents on income support before they went to university, and which they continued to experience in some of their interactions with university life.

The vocational orientation of the students in this study further indicated their desire for inclusion. Their orientation to use their education to benefit their children and the wider community seemed to resonate with the observations of both Gilligan (1982) and Belenky *et al* (1986), that women:

> . . . are drawn to the role of caretaker and nurturer, often putting their
> own needs at the bottom of the list . . . (Belenky *et al* 1986, p. 77)

Sandra and Hazel both strongly articulated a desire to make a positive impact in their communities, to make a contribution to society and to gain sufficient self-respect to help them make a positive difference to other people's lives. Their problem was that they struggled to achieve this at considerable personal and economic cost, and that the support for their efforts was so inadequate.

I HAVE LEARNED A LOT ABOUT MYSELF: LEARNING FOR JENNY

Jenny's course in community and youth work involved a practical place-ment and group work, as well as attending more formal lectures and seminars. She expressed her learning in terms of her increased self-awareness:

> I've learned a lot about myself and how I see myself, and how other people see me, and the implications of what I might say. How it can help or not help how people see me. How I view things. It's changed. They did tell us it would change and I just laughed. I just thought: I don't think so. But I have changed. I think I have.

Jenny saw herself a less selfish, more open person:

> Before it was – I was all about self, self, self. I really didn't care about other people. Well, I did, but I wasn't going to take on any-body's problems when I've got my own. Now, I'm more accessible, more open. I will listen; and listening was one of my weaknesses. I didn't want to listen for too long. It was too boring. Now I will listen because it's interesting listening to other people and listening to their views and how they see things. It can help you. That's what I've learned. Yes, I do listen. I like to hear what people say now, because I was too quick to put my views in . . . College helped. Listening to other people, their views and their values.

Jenny saw her placement experience as crucial to her changing atti-tudes:

> I had to put others first and be prepared to compromise – which I was never prepared to do. But my placement changed that. When you have to meet people, you're going to work with different people for X amount of time, you've got to learn to listen to them. You might not like what they say; at the end of the day, you might not go ahead with what they say, but you bear it in mind. At some point you'll come to some common ground.

She summarised what she saw as the lessons of community work practice:

> You've always got to keep at the back of your mind where you are and what you're doing, and why you're there, and what it's all about. You could easily go off and do your own thing . . . If you just stay focused on what you're doing and what it's all about – and who you're there for.

UNIVERSITY CHANGES YOUR WAY OF THINKING: LEARNING FOR GLORIA

Gloria was doing a degree in Childhood Studies, which involved studying History and English. She was enthusiastic about particular aspects of her studies.

> Very interesting. Everyday issues such as the Welfare State. Issues that you were aware of but you don't really understand.

English in particular filled her with enthusiasm because of the enthusiasm of the lecturer:

> The lecturer is very witty, sensitive and enthusiastic. He's very aware of the need to express culture, and this comes across in his lectures. Also, we explored literature from different angles, not just from an English perspective. We've also looked at black American writers as well. It has been really fascinating. For example, an inspirational writer such as Nella Larsen – born in the 1920s. She looked at race from a mixed parentage point of view. She addresses the issue of 'passing'. She opposes the minority who live in self-denial of history, to pass as Caucasoid. It was of interest, because it was something that my mother could relate to. You see my mother derived from the West Indies and her mother was of mixed race. My mother once told me a story of some cousins that went to America, and because they were of mixed race and when they married they did not want their wives to know that their ancestry was black . . . it made me wonder whether 'passing' was more common than thought.We also looked at writers and poets such as Oscar Wilde and Sylvia Plath. And although I've heard of William Shakespeare, I don't think it was one of those subjects I would have found interesting if I had not had such an enthusiastic lecturer.

For Gloria memorable learning was achieved when she was able to make connections with her own life and experiences:

> Yes, university changes your way of thinking. For example, the childhood studies course for me has opened up a whole new world to the history of childhood. Having found out through the course that prior to the nineteenth century, childhood for children in England was a limited period of subordination and then they became little adults . . . These are things that we take for granted. Also that during this century, childhood can also depend on where a person lives. Yes, it has really enhanced my outlook on life. It has definitely left me with food for thought.

Learning experiences

From students' descriptions of their learning it was striking how seldom it was expressed in academic terms or in terms of what had been learned in the lecture room. Most often, learning arose from practice, or from making connections between their own lives and experiences and curriculum content. For those, like Helen, Sandra, Jenny and Hazel who were on courses of professional training, learning was generally described in the context of their experience on practical placement. For Helen and Jenny learning was about knowing themselves better, about recognising weaknesses and working positively upon them. Learning in theory arose from learning in practice, and rarely the other way round. Each of these women had earlier mentioned the difficulties they had with reading, with expressing themselves in writing and with understanding theory. However, their descriptions of their learning in practice (Lave and Wenger 1991) demonstrated their growing ability to reflect on experience and to elaborate on the importance of concepts such as self-knowledge, stereotyping and professionalism.

Gloria, Seima and Baljit were studying on degree courses which they had chosen because they were geared towards teaching. However, they were not courses of professional training, and therefore did not include periods of practical placement experience. The learning which they recalled particularly vividly related directly to their own lives. Seima and Gloria both remembered the same session in their course, a lecture on the history of childhood, as a learning experience. Both had been struck and surprised that the concept of childhood was a relatively new one. Both had drawn comparisons between their own children's lives and those of children in different time and geographical contexts. Gloria's most potent memory of learning, which she described at length and in detail, linked her own experience as a black woman of historically mixed heritage with the literature of the African-American novelist, Nella Larsen (1986). The lecturer who taught the class which Gloria described was, from her point of view, an enthusiastic and able teacher, a view which was independently echoed by Baljit. This lecturer had enabled Gloria to make connections between her own experience and academic work in a way no other student had described. That the link related to race was particularly striking, given Gloria's and others' accounts of the silencing of the race issue in classroom discussion.

Connected learning

The gains of higher education were seen in terms of a greater awareness of the wider world, an enhanced sense of self, and a feeling of improved social status. Learning was seen as being connected to personal experience, either through the practical aspects of a course, or through students being able to make a link between the personal and the academic. Wenger (1998) has described this as education 'in its deepest sense', which:

> Concerns the opening of identities – exploring new ways of being that lie beyond our current state. (p. 263)

Participants rarely described their own learning as arising from the teaching of theory, or abstract subject matter. Learning seemed to take place when they engaged in situations which had relevance to their own lives. This perspective on learning calls into question what is taken for granted in the institutional structure and practices of higher education: that learning is achieved solely by formal teaching (Bowden and Marton 1998). It also questions a number of other assumptions about how learning takes place:

> Our institutions, to the extent that they address the issue of learning explicitly, are largely based on the assumption that learning is an individual process, that it has a beginning and an end, that it is best separated from the rest of our activities, and that it is a result of teaching. (Wenger 1998, p. 3)

From the point of view of our students, the learning process was very different. Learning was not purely an individual process; it involved interaction. In Helen's case, it involved interacting with a group of people hitherto unknown to her, whom she had previously viewed through society's stereotyping lens as dangerous and difficult. In Jenny's case, it entailed learning to listen to others, to look at situations from their perspective, and to subordinate her own needs. For Gloria, Baljit and Seima, the learning they recalled from lectures was not separate from, but strongly connected to the rest of their lives – to their current role as parent, and to their past history. Learning was seen as not necessarily a result of teaching but rather of making connections between their own lives and aspects of their courses.

Belenky *et al* (1986) have characterised the type of learning described by these participants as 'connected knowing' which, although not gender specific, appeared to them to be gender related:

> Connected knowers develop procedures for gaining access to other people's knowledge. At the heart of these procedures is the capacity for empathy. Since knowledge comes from experience, the only way they can hope to understand another person's ideas is to try to share the experience that has led the person to form the idea. (p. 113)

From their study of *Women's Ways of Knowing*, they noted numerous instances of women, particularly in their first year of study, describing learning in the 'connected' sense that Gloria, Helen, Baljit and Jenny describe it. They go on to argue that such knowing:

> . . . grows out of the experience of relationships; it requires intimacy and equality between self and object, not distance and impersonality; its goal is understanding, not proof. (p. 183)

As women, these students often stressed their alienation from academic modes of teaching, expectations and conventions which are largely male-defined. Their opportunities to make connections between their lives as parents and their lives as learners were limited by their need to separate their personal worlds from academia. As black and Asian women, an entire aspect of their lives was often denied in the classroom by the defensive tactics of their white fellow students. Therefore it is not surprising that descriptions of academic or theory learning within the university were few and far between. The research shows a sharp contrast between their efforts to work for their own social inclusion, and the confusion, isolation and alienation which they experienced in their contact with the system. It raises questions about whether the rhetoric of widening participation means anything to these working class, ethnic minority mature students. These questions will be explored in both a theoretical and practical context in Part Two.

Part Two

PARADOXES IN WIDENING
PARTICIPATION

8

THE UNEVEN PLAYING FIELD IN EDUCATION

The government's saying: we want you to move forwards, get a proper qualification, get a job. I think we've tried that. There's always something to shove you back.

Sandra: Social Work student

I think they just want to keep the status quo. And I think they might be taking on a few mature students because they can say: 'Oh, we've got a few mature students – we take mature students'.

Salma: Social Policy student

Some contradictions

The language of education at the beginning of the twenty-first century resonates with the terminology of inclusion. Why then did the students in this study, who were positively oriented towards education and the benefits it could bring, experience themselves as outsiders in education? And why, when they finally managed to break through into higher education, did they experience it as alienating and confusing? It could be that these negative experiences are just part of the process of transition. Perhaps we are currently in transition from elite to inclusive education, which requires only technical and administrative adjustments for its achievement. The outcome of this research suggests that this is not the case.

Evidence from interviews and discussion with the research participants over a period of more than three years indicated that their experiences prior to entering higher education were marked by lack of information, support and guidance, and by missing opportunities to obtain the educational, financial and social advantages of degree level success. They were *frustrated participants* – educational activists rather than non-participants, who had in the past tried unsuccessfully to negotiate the obstacles in their path, and who had concluded that higher education was not for people like them. However, they were prepared to keep trying and, with the support and guidance which Reachout offered, they managed to gain access to university.

The majority of those who did enter higher education experienced their first year as a continuing struggle against economic, institutional and social constraints and felt a sense of exclusion. Nevertheless they believed that higher education would bring eventual rewards and that it was therefore worth persevering. However, they took it upon themselves to try to resolve the contradictions between the demands of the institution and the demands of the real world. The role and structure of the educational institutions was not questioned. Although students did find ways of coping with the contradictions of university life, its demands and its underlying purpose were frequently at odds with their own. Whilst there appears to be a sense in which non-traditional students do accommodate themselves to the rigours and expectations of university life (Merrill 1999), the evidence of this study is that this is frequently achieved at the expense of their personal, cultural, social and economic well-being. Furthermore, issues of gender, class and especially race, which were silenced within academic life, still impacted negatively upon them and prevented their views from being aired in formal learning situations.

An analysis of some of the structural constraints acting upon them may help us to move from individuals' anecdotal accounts of their struggles with the system towards seeing non-traditional students' careers as being affected by wider social and cultural factors which affect equality issues. The following two chapters utilise two theoretical frameworks.

The first, Bourdieu's (1966, 1977, 1979, 1997) analysis throws light on why those from working class and ethnic minority backgrounds find themselves outsiders in this game: why they are ruled out of making progress and how they conclude that they themselves have contributed to their own exclusion. The second, that of Michael Apple (1986, 1990, 1991, 1993) helps us to explore in more detail the way in which exclusion works in the everyday practices of university life.

A hidden curriculum of lack of support

Throughout their lives, it seemed that our students had failed to benefit from the information, guidance and support available to younger students from middle class backgrounds. Failure to receive support affected them at all stages in their educational careers, from school, to careers guidance and on to university. Much of this support (for example, parental knowledge of educational opportunities and options) is so taken for granted that it is hard to see, unless a close look is taken at the way in which non-traditional students struggle to find their way through to higher education. Some of these students, had they been brought up in other social settings, would have known how to overcome the setbacks they met in their school careers. They might have been able to retake failed examinations or have chosen college courses which were more likely to be accepted by universities. They might have known that the earlier qualifications they had gained at college would be accepted by some universities and that they did not need to restart their studies from scratch. Those who did eventually go on to university were failed again by the hidden curriculum of university life. They found themselves unable to understand its tacit requirements or to take advantage of the informal support networks available to younger, middle class students whose social focus is the university campus. Whilst many students, whatever their background, may find that university life does not offer the support they anticipated our students had few alternative sources of help.

Relative poverty of money, time and goods

More glaringly obvious, as participants entered higher education, was their disadvantaged position in relation to students who were younger, and therefore more likely to cope with the debt which now comes with university study. These younger students had a degree of financial security which accrued from their class and family background, and did not have children or family responsibilities. In particular, the stories of the full-time students were dominated by a sense of desperation about making ends meet for themselves and their children. Their relative poverty, reinforced by the knowledge that they lacked the books, computers and other hardware associated with university study in the twenty-first century, made their initiation into higher education difficult and potentially isolating.

Power imbalances

At university, there were imbalances of power between tutors and students which seemed inappropriate in the context of adults working together. Students who, like Ruth, felt that the situation should be one of power sharing, were deeply disappointed when they found that the power balance was very much as they had experienced it at school, with the added difficulty that the culture and norms of higher education were a mystery to them. These students did not know the rules of the game of university life. They often felt that they were working in the dark, trying to give tutors what they wanted, but without a clear idea of what exactly this should be. They expressed a sense of powerlessness in the face of the institution, whose rules were implicit, rather than explicit. At university, as at school, they felt themselves to be marked out as different. Being in a minority because of their age, class and race made them feel vulnerable and powerless.

Self-blame

With striking regularity, they blamed themselves for their failure to make earlier educational progress and for their initial failure to get a grip on university life and its demands. At school, difficulties in getting teacher support and careers information were interpreted as cultural or family failings. At university, difficulties in coping with complex child-care arrangements and unaccommodating timetables were interpreted as poor time management. Difficulties with understanding what was required of them in completing assignment tasks were interpreted as lack of intelligence or education, compared with younger A-Level students. It seemed that they had internalised their own disadvantage and turned it against themselves. They blamed themselves for the failure of the educational institutions to offer them support, to make their studies manageable, and to provide guidance about the rules of academic performance.

The uneven playing field

The research showed that there was an uneven playing field in education; that these students were constantly engaged in an uphill struggle; that the odds were stacked against them from the outset and that the system within which they were trying to survive and succeed was structurally unfair. Bourdieu (1966, 1977, 1979, 1997) has analysed educational inequality through his discussion of habitus and capital. Bourdieu's analysis helps to explain the paradox of governmental and institutional rhetoric on widening participation against a background of continued inequality of representation and experience for those who have been targeted as the beneficiaries of social inclusion.

Field, habitus and capital

Bourdieu (1966) describes education as a 'field', an identifiable and structured set of relations within which social activity is reproduced through discourse. Within this framework, higher education is a sub-field, linked to other branches of education (such as secondary school, careers and employment services), and to other fields (such as the unemployment and benefits system and occupational structures) but with its own particular set of social relations. Habitus, 'history turned into nature' (Bourdieu 1977, p. 78), refers to the way in which individual thought and activity interact with the field to maintain, through tacit rules, norms and traditions, the structure and relations of the field or sub-field. In doing so, a field, or an institution within a field, tends to reproduce and maintain itself. The strength of habitus in maintaining and reproducing existing institutional relations is that those subject to it do not necessarily feel the weight of the rules laid upon them:

> When habitus encounters a social world of which it is the product, it finds itself as a 'fish in water', it does not feel the weight of the water and takes the world about itself for granted. (Bourdieu 1989, cited in Grenfell and James 1998, p. 14)

The habitus related to educational practices and policies may be unthinking, taken for granted, habitual. It could be argued that this explains the apparent contradiction between an institutional language which speaks of inclusion, and educational experiences which appear to exclude ethnic minority pupils from working class backgrounds and university students who do not fit the standard profile of the under-graduate: eighteen-year-old, white and middle class. It might also provide an explanatory framework for the apparent lack of significant change in institutional practices to take account of the rhetoric. Viewed in this light, the processes and practices of higher education become a 'game' with both explicit and implicit rules, but a game whose defining principles are never made entirely clear to those who enter it from outside:

> By entering the game, individuals implicitly agree to be ruled by it and immediately set up personal relations with it, as well as other players. (Grenfell and James 1998, p. 18)

In Bourdieu's framework, everyone is apparently free to play the game of education, and to receive its rewards. But differentials in habitus ensure that not everyone plays the game on equal terms: the playing field is not a level one. Individuals come to the game with differences in their knowledge of its rules, and having already gained different rewards in other spheres, such as in earlier education, in family life, or in financial and material resources. The winners in the education game are those who accrue its prizes, be they actual (in the form of qualifications and jobs) or symbolic (in the form of increased status or self-esteem). However, the unevenness of the playing field is evident in that some already had prizes on entry to the game, and will therefore be likely to carry more prizes away at the end.

Such prizes are *capital* which may be accrued before, during or after the process of higher education. Bourdieu's discussion of the concept of capital in relation to the process and outcomes of education may help to provide explanations for the differential benefits gained from education, according to differences in class, gender, race and age. The accumulation of capital is the outcome of the game of education. However, capital is not just reducible to economic holdings. Nor is capital always concrete and objectifiable, it may be symbolic, and thus reliant on habitus for its maintenance. Bourdieu (1997) distinguishes three forms of capital: economic, cultural and social. He defines each form:

... capital can present itself in three fundamental guises: as economic capital, which is immediately and directly convertible into money and may be institutionalised in the form of property rights; as cultural capital, which is convertible, on certain conditions, into economic capital and may be institutionalised in the form of educational qualifications; and as social capital, made up of social obligations ('connections'), which is convertible, in certain conditions, into economic capital and may be institutionalised in the form of a title of nobility. (Bourdieu 1997, p. 47)

For Bourdieu, the possession of economic capital is fundamental to all aspects of the game of education, as indeed this study has shown. Lack of economic capital is partly what had kept our student group away from believing that education is accessible to them. Scarcity of economic capital while studying is a major factor in making the experience of higher education an intensely difficult one. The desire to accrue economic capital for themselves and their children was the main motivation for most of the group to strive for admission to higher education:

So it has to be posited simultaneously that economic capital is at the root of all other types of capital and that these transformed, disguised forms of economic capital . . . produce their most specific effects only to the extent that they conceal the fact that economic capital is at their root. (Bourdieu 1997, p. 54)

However, differences in educational experiences and outcomes are not only economically influenced. There are social and cultural forms of capital which can indirectly be exchanged for economic advancement.

Bourdieu (1997, p. 187) cites three states in which cultural capital may exist. First, in embodied form, it is exemplified in features of the individual which are construed as having value, such as accent, familiarity with academic discourse or the appearance of being cultured. Second, it can exist in the objectified state, in the form of cultural goods, such as books, instruments and machines. Finally, it can exist in the institutionalised state, particularly in the form of qualifications bestowed by educational institutions, which may be transformed directly into economic capital, in the shape of well paid work.

Although more hidden and indirect in its effects, the transmission of cultural capital can be seen as crucial to the process of social reproduction.

In fact, it is the hidden nature of cultural capital, particularly in its embodied form, which makes it so powerful. It can operate alongside opposing policies of inclusion and equality. It can be confused with heredity, and therefore avoid being blamed for the perpetuation of educational and occupational inequality. Time is an important factor in the ability to accumulate institutional cultural capital. The longer you have at your disposal, the easier it becomes to acquire the necessary qualifications through the acquisition of study habits which lead to valued levels of qualification. Thus, in the sphere of education, those who can afford the time to retake failed exams, whose families can afford to pay for extra years at school and private tuition are more likely to gain the qualifications which will move them on economically.

Bourdieu has described social capital as:

> ... the aggregate of potential resources which are linked to possession of a durable network of more or less institutionalized relationships of mutual acquaintance and recognition – or in other words, to membership in a group. (Bourdieu 1997, p. 51)

The possession of social capital involves the development of networks which provide back-up and affirmation of social position – in common parlance the old boy network or the old school tie. When used derogatorily, it refers to the use of educational, family or employer networks to gain and maintain economic or social advantage. It is a key aspect of modern day practices such as networking in the academic and professional field and head hunting in the employment field.

For those whose family has traditionally experienced university education, holdings of social capital in the field of education are likely to be greater than for those without this background. Such social capital can provide access to information, advice, connections and, ultimately well paid careers. From the research it was apparent that for those students whose parents were educated outside the United Kingdom there were clear gaps in their educational social networks, and hence in access to sources of formal and informal help and information. This lack of access to social and information networks has also been noted in other areas of education (Reay 1998).

Self-blame: internalising the message of exclusion

Habitus exerts an influence on individual decision-making in organizational contexts by creating a common set of expectations of appropriate college choices that limits the universe of possible colleges into a smaller range of manageable considerations. (McDonough 1995, p. 182)

When comparing working class and middle class parents' involvement in their children's schooling, Reay (1998) noted the tendency for middle class parents to locate the cause of their children's educational difficulties in the school, whereas working class parents tended to blame either themselves or their children for any educational problems which arose. Thus it was with the students in this study. The research revealed that there were ways in which, through internalising institutional exclusionary attitudes and practices, they saw themselves as less worthy, or less able than their fellow students. It also revealed a tendency for them to make choices based on their sense of exclusion from higher status education. Bourdieu and Passeron (1977, p. 41) have described how those who are excluded from education 'internalize the legitimacy of their own exclusion', and thus come to accept that certain types of education are superior in terms of the cultural capital they accrue, but are reserved for others and not for them. In doing so, they relegate themselves to forms of education which are less valued and which carry less cultural, and ultimately less economic, capital. These tendencies made themselves felt at all levels in the process of moving towards higher education: in the students' acceptance of their limited career and educational options, in course and university choice, and in their view of their performance in academic life when they started at university.

Other writers too, (Robbins 1993, Reay 1995) have noted the tendency for habitus to operate in such a way that working class people may not think they are eligible for opportunities to achieve because of their internalised assumptions that certain opportunities are 'not for the likes of them'. Our student group appeared to be well aware of the differential status of higher education institutions. Their perception of their own status in relation to these institutions affected their choice of study location. Although Bourdieu (1977, p. 187), in discussing the cultural capital embodied in French qualifications, talks of a 'single market' in which a certain level of qualification has a fixed value, which can be exchanged for economic capital, this appears not to be quite the case in the current UK system of higher education.

In 1992, former polytechnics were given university status and, in theory at least, a unified system of higher education was established, which also acknowledged the need for diversity (Jary and Parker 1998). It is evident, however, that there is a status divide in higher education between the new (post-1992) and the old (pre-1992) universities. There is also a status divide between the universities and the colleges of higher education. Different terms have been used to label institutions and thus, indirectly, indicate their differential status. Among these labels have been: research versus teaching universities, pre-1992 versus post-1992 universities, traditional versus non-traditional universities, ancient versus modern universities and Russell Group universities versus the rest. James (1995) has drawn attention to the differential holdings of cultural capital of different institutions. The labels placed upon them affect their reputation in the eyes of students. The students in this study, although relative novices to the higher education game, quickly became aware of the status of different higher education institutions, and were usually drawn towards those with perceived lower academic and social status.

When they did eventually reach the point at which university entry might be a possibility, the majority of participants, who were mature, working class, black and Asian women, consciously opted to go to less prestigious universities because they sensed that they would feel more comfortable and less conspicuous there. They were aware, however, that this might mean gaining qualifications which were less highly valued in the job market. Hence these students deliberately chose to attend colleges and universities which held less cultural capital, and so slotted into their perceived place in the structure of higher education. For Salma, who had weighed up university status against the likelihood of exclusion, and decided to opt for the higher status university, exclusion was keenly felt. Her experience led her to advise others not to make the same choice as herself. Internalised messages about the status of different institutions affected the choices which participants felt able to make.

Once at university, a further set of messages were received about the students' ability to live up to its academic expectations. Bourdieu and Passeron (1977) have discussed the role of language in French higher education in creating and reinforcing the distance between university teachers and their students, academic discourse and the communication of ideas being almost mutually exclusive. However, students have to maintain a pretence of understanding. If a student admits to a failure to understand something, it is her fault. Blaming her for not understanding reinforces her sense of inadequacy at failing to grasp academic language – a language which, as Bourdieu and Passeron state, has never been anyone's mother tongue.

Bourdieu's analysis of habitus and capital provides a way of examining how advantage and disadvantage operate within education, not only in relation to class, but to race, gender and age. It helps to explain why those who have been identified as non-traditional on more than one count, although they may not share the same criteria, are likely to share the experience of exclusion . It also helps to explain why they may even be led to define themselves and as unworthy or blameworthy and to act in ways which reinforce their disadvantage. The following chapter explores how the well worn practices and assumptions of education operate to maintain the status quo and perpetuate the sense of exclusion amongst those who do eventually break through into higher education.

9
EXCLUSIONARY PRACTICES IN HIGHER EDUCATION

I've felt I've been left out because I've got no knowledge.
Salma: Social Policy student

Whose knowledge is it? Who selected it? Why is it organised and taught in this way? To this particular group?
Apple 1990, p. 7

Michael Apple (1990) has divided his examination of education's relationship to structures of power and domination into three parts: institutional, curricular and pedagogic. Such clear cut divisions are artificial but serve to illustrate the ways in which different aspects of educational policy and practice operate to maintain exclusion. From the perspective of those involved in this research, there also seemed to be institutional, curricular and pedagogic ways in which the university, other institutions and the wider environment operated to perpetuate their exclusion within higher education, even when the illusion of inclusion was present.

Institutional manifestations of exclusionary practice

Higher education institutions may be regarded as storehouses of cultural capital, acting as a means of reproducing a hierarchical society

(Bourdieu 1997). The culture constituted through white, male, middle class norms is taken as containing natural, fixed and unquestionable assumptions. These assumptions are based on a concept of educational success which is dependent on individual, examination based achievement, and on the idea that students should come, ready formed, to the university, able to stand on their own feet from day one, without expectation of support from the institution itself.

A-Level students entering higher education straight from school are likely to measure up to these assumptions more easily because when they were at school they were able to devote time to developing the habitus and accruing the cultural capital they need to operate within the institution. Once in higher education, they have more time and opportunity to assume the cultural mores of the institution. Also, the modes of learning generally employed in A-Level work are more likely to coincide with those of the university, involving individual essay writing and examinations, as opposed to the more experiential and group work based styles of teaching and learning frequently adopted on Access Courses.

Halls of residence, student communal living and time for socialising outside classes provide a supportive framework for the eighteen year old. The availability of university facilities close at hand and ready access to academic discourse on site provide an easy bridge between school and university life. In contrast, the mature, home-based student with family responsibilities has less time and space, both at university and at home, to internalise the language and norms of the university. Also, she is likely to be less familiar with such norms, based as they are on elite concepts of learning and achievement through individual, rather than collective endeavour.

There appear to be two inbuilt assumptions within the framework of higher education about the time available to students: the first that it is fairly limitless, the second that it is relatively flexible. For the students in this study, neither of these assumptions were correct. They have been described as time poor; they tried constantly to appease the demands of the 'greedy institutions' (Edwards 1993) while still giving their families, and particularly their children, the quality of care they feel they deserved. Frequently, the study time which should have been available to them was spent working to meet the financial demands of maintaining home and children. Constraints on students' finances mean that many students, whether straight from school or not, are compelled to undertake paid work in order to keep the level of their debts manageable (Haselgrove 1994).

A further set of assumptions are those based on a male view of family responsibility. Reay (1998) has pointed out that the habitus of higher education is not just class based. It is also gendered. It therefore tends to render aspects of women's experience, both within and outside the institution, invisible. University and college practice and culture rarely take more than token account of the caring responsibilities of its students. Evidence from this study and others (for example, Merrill 1999) shows that concessions around the timing of classes to fit in with childcare and family responsibilities are generally made on an individual, or small group basis, rather than being matters of institutional policy. In this study, students with children described having to negotiate leaving lectures early to collect their children from school or nursery. Such flexibility was rarely offered in advance. From the students' viewpoints, asking for time concessions around childcare was likely to be perceived as an indication of weakness or awkwardness on their part, so they were often reluctant to ask.

There were also institutional assumptions about the amount of object related cultural capital (Bourdieu 1997, p. 50) possessed by students in this study: their ownership of books, access to a computer for word-processing assignments, and the availability of study space at home. For almost all the students these assumptions were completely unfounded. Apple (1986) observed the possible impact of the introduction of technology into education in the United States. He saw advantages accruing to middle class students from their access to computer owner-ship and knowledge, which gave them the prospect of greater mobility and economic gain in times of economic crisis. This research study revealed that technological disadvantages were particularly acute for these students when they began their university studies. They did not have access to computers at home, and could not afford the time to stay at university to use the on-site facilities. Buying books was also a matter of weighing up family priorities against institutional expectations. Time and space at home were often hard won. Reading had to be done wherever and whenever time could be found. Students' difficulties in obtaining the material symbols of higher education and the time to study had the effect of creating further isolation.

The institutional habitus carries with it assumptions about access to money, time and resources. It is also gendered, to the extent that it does not formally acknowledge the reality of women's lives as parents and carers and workers.

Curricular forms of exclusion

Wright (1989) has drawn attention to the conflict between wanting to make higher education more accessible to students from a wider range of backgrounds, and higher education's existing subject matter, language, power relations and means of measuring attainment. He has observed that the further removed the content and procedures of higher education are from everyday experience, the more likely those who achieve within it are to be socially distanced from, and to enjoy social and political power over, those who do not.

The students in this study were almost exclusively drawn to social science or people centred areas of the higher education curriculum, which appear to be areas close to 'everyday thought and experience' (Wright 1989, p. 101). These areas include psychology, sociology, social policy, social and community work, childhood studies and teaching. For a number of reasons this is not surprising. Most students stated that their orientation to study was vocational rather than academic. Being older, they were concerned to enter work as soon as they could. They therefore chose to study the subjects most likely to lead on to employment. Most of the participants were women and their career aspirations were strongly influenced by gender expectations – careers in the caring professions or teaching which were compatible with part time working and school holiday commitments. A third reason may have been that these areas of study are thought to be more favourably disposed towards adult students with non-traditional qualifications. This may reflect the relatively low status of these subject areas in the academic world, and hence their need to open up to a wider range of students to keep numbers up (Sanders 2000).

One of the challenges of teaching in the social sciences is that it is possible to build on students' everyday experience and understanding of the world, and to link this understanding to theoretical analysis. It is also more possible for the methods of teaching and learning to encourage students to question accepted forms of knowledge than in other areas of study. However, as Apple (1990) has observed, there are ways in which even a social science curriculum can be depoliticised and rendered neutral. A number of examples from the research study illustrate this.

Social and community work courses stress that anti-discriminatory and empowering practice is fundamental to the curriculum (Dominelli 1988, CCETSW 1991, Adams 1993, Hugman and Smith 1995, Barnes and Warren (eds) 1999). Students on these courses are expected to examine and challenge their own prejudices to find out how oppression works and to reflect on how they, as professionals, might consciously or unconsciously act to perpetuate oppression. Almost all assignment tasks within social and community work require students to integrate anti-oppressive practice into their responses. However, in day to day class-room discussion, black students on these courses reported that their attempts to raise issues of discrimination were either sabotaged or silenced by white students. Thus, although there was a theoretical com-mitment to anti-oppressive practice, and a clearly stated expectation that students would develop it, there was no expectaton that this would be carried through into classroom interaction and group learning. Nor did strategies appear to have been developed to allow conflict to be acknowledged and dealt with to promote change.

Likewise, the aim of empowerment, although a course requirement in theory, did not seem to be expected in practice. In the area of social work, the concept of empowerment directly conflicts with the social worker's legislative role, which may involve taking away the liberty of those who are diagnosed mentally ill, or taking children into care with-out the consent of their parents. The empowering role of the social worker conflicts with her role as an agent of social control. Although students were expected to link theory with practice in assessed work, these issues tended not to be addressed and discussed within the curri-culum itself. The contrast between theory and practice was evident in the students' experiences. In both community work and social work training, the ideal of empowerment seemed to be at odds with the students' own experiences on their courses, where they felt powerless to challenge the prevailing white liberal hegemony of the institution, or to question judgements made about their work which confused and alienated them.

In social policy, too, there appeared to be a failure to take account of and make links between the curriculum content and students' real life experiences. The most striking example of this was in Salma's case, where teaching about the subject matter of poverty took place without reference to the way in which a university, its departments and staff themselves might be contributing to the exclusion and marginalisation of a student living in poverty. Once more, the student is silenced, opposition is suppressed, and criticism of day to day exclusionary practice is sidelined.

Apple (1990) has discussed the way in which the school curriculum in the United States assumes ideological consensus, and leaves little room for dealing with issues of conflict or contradiction based on class, race or gender. It is therefore not surprising that both the overt and covert curriculum suppress conflict in favour of a liberal notion of consensus in which:

> . . . considerations of the justice of social life are progressively depoliticized and made into a supposedly neutral puzzle that can be solved by the accumulation of neutral empirical facts. (Apple 1990, p. 8)

In this study too, terms used in the curriculum content of university courses – such as disempowerment, oppression and poverty were reduced to simple theoretical constructs, rather than being recognised as a part of the lived experience of the students. It was striking that a number of participants said that race issues were suppressed in class discussion, that differences between black students' and white students' perspectives were left only partially discussed and therefore unresolved. Sandra, Hazel and Helen certainly concluded that race and racism were 'no go areas' in class discussion.

Another aspect of the curriculum which reinforced their sense of exclusion was the relationship between what was taught and the way in which it was assessed. The separation of the process of teaching from that of assessment manifested itself in what students saw as the unwillingness of teaching staff to guide and comment on their efforts to complete assessed work, in case it compromised their role as assessors. A view of assessment as an individual, summative activity, as testing rather than developing skills and exploring ideas, was thus fostered. For those students in the study who did not come from a traditional, exam-based A-Level background, this situation was exacerbated by confusion about what was required for successful assessment. Students frequently stated that they did not fully understand the expectations of academic work. 'What do they want?' was a question asked by a number of those interviewed, and this question has been echoed in other accounts of students' experiences of higher education (see for example, Merrill 1999, p. 142).

The language of higher education was assumed to be neutral by those within the system. If a student did not understand what was required, she felt that this would be construed as her failure to meet (unspecified) academic standards, rather than a failure on the part of the institution to help the student to comprehend and evaluate the worth of academic language:

> The majority of students and pupils encounter the language use of the educational knowledge code as Other. Learning the rules of how to perform properly and acceptably is a painful and difficult procedure. (Livingstone 1987, p. 31)

Language and ways of expressing oneself are, within Bourdieu's (1997) framework, vital aspects of embodied cultural capital. The language of academic life is taken as a given; failure to understand or speak it is taken as educational deficit, which the student must remedy or leave.

The evidence of this research revealed that once in higher education, our student group felt that they were expected to assimilate, almost by osmosis, the academic requirements of the institution. Yet these requirements were often implicit rather than explicit, and even lengthy assignment titles and tasks did not necessarily explain what was expected. Both the overt and covert aspects of the curriculum operated in such a way that participants felt inadequate. For example, they had difficulty in understanding academic language, which they saw as 'their' problem.

The external doors of academia may have been opened, but the internal doors which might reveal the expectations of the academy remained closed, and the concerns of students' own lives, experienced through discrimination, poverty and the responsibilities of parenthood, were excluded from discussion, even when they were highly relevant to the taught curriculum. The constituency of higher education may have been changing but its habitus appeared to have remained more or less intact.

Educators' roles in exclusionary practice

The way in which they experience their relationship with lecturers and their lectures, and tutors and their tutorials is central to students' academic lives. In this research study these relationships were characterised by unequal power, mystification and distancing from students' academic and personal concerns. Teachers appear to have a complex role in maintaining hegemony, through their position as relatively powerful people within the process of economic, social and cultural reproduction (Bowles and Gintis 1976), and as workers who are relatively powerless in relation to the prevailing ideology of education (Apple 1986, 1993).

As relatively powerful people, school teachers and careers advisors can, through a process of stereotyping and labelling, channel young people into particular areas, limit their aspirations and reinforce their sense of exclusion (Sharpe 1976, Delamont 1980, Measor and Sikes 1992). This study has demonstrated that in higher education, they can foster isolation and individualism and reinforce the hierarchical nature of education, through mystification of the teaching and assessment process. They can refuse to guide students as to whether they are interpreting an essay title correctly, as in Sandra's case, or they can distance themselves from the concerns of students, as in Salma's case. They can also label their students as problematic or abnormal because of the nature of their qualifications on entry. Tutors can intensify students' sense of inadequacy as learners, and contribute to their demoralisation by social categorising. On more than one occasion, students in the study recounted being negatively labelled as 'Access Students', an indication that they were not in higher education by right but because of their disadvantaged status, which made them less likely to be able to meet its requirements. However, evidence has shown this presumed inadequacy to be untrue (Smithers and Griffin 1986).

Inequality of power relations between teacher and student was a factor in some students' negative relationships with academic staff. For mature students, where the age difference between student and teacher was either negligible or where teachers are younger than their students, problems of power differentials tended to be expressed in a number of ways. Some students were reluctant to approach tutors with problems, fearing that they would be found inadequate and forced to leave; tutors and lecturers were seen as lofty, inaccessible and uninterested in students' concerns. Students involved in this study, and particularly those who took part in the *Students Speak* conference, thought that the student-tutor relationship should be characterised by power-sharing, rather than power inequality.

Aside from the part teachers may unwittingly play in maintaining white middle class hegemony, there is also a way in which, as members of the working class, they are prevented by the rules of the system from developing more emancipatory forms of teaching and more supportive roles in relation to their students' efforts to understand the tacit rules of academic life (Cotterill and Waterhouse 1998). University teachers have been subject to divisive and market oriented policies imposed by governments bent on centralising, standardising and controlling educational output (Apple 1993).

The separation of research and teaching functions in higher education and the consequent downgrading of teaching have increased the distance between university teachers and their students (Jary and Parker 1998). New Right ideals of managerialism and of the prioritisation of technology over human contact have had an impact on education which seems to have continued well after the demise of the Conservative government. James (1998) describes an aspect of his own study of the connection between teaching, research and student experience. He reports first year students' high levels of dissatisfaction with teaching and seminars, which was expressed by both experienced and inexperienced entrants to higher education. It appeared to dissipate over time, however, as students recognised some of the constraints under which teachers worked, such as the pressure to research and publish, or as they became part of the culture of university life and lowered their expectations of its teaching.

James (1998) talked to university teachers about their own views on the relative priorities of teaching and research within their institution. What became clear was that the priorities within the field of higher education and, consequently, the habitus of academic staff, was to devalue pedagogy in favour of research. University research carries with it greater economic and symbolic capital than teaching. Teaching is described as coming fourth in a list of priorities, referred to as P.R.A.T. by one student in James' study as

> . . . it's publish . . . research, admin work and teaching is four.
> (James, in Grenfell and James 1998, p. 112)

If teaching comes low down on the list of priorities, the teaching of first year students is likely to be given even lower status. It is less likely to enable the lecturer to talk about their own research interests and carries even less symbolic capital than other undergraduate teaching. From his interview data, James constructs the elements of an 'ideal lecture':

> . . . which included such features as lecturer enthusiasm, student participation, clear signposting and the clear display of key terms.
> (James in Grenfell and James 1998, p. 111)

From this study, it was clear that as far as first year students were concerned, good lecturing was the exception rather than the rule. Lecturers were perceived as pursuing their own interests outside and inside the lecture theatre, and as regarding lecturing as a chore that had low priority. It was up to the student to make of it what she could.

James (1998) and Merrill (1999) have observed that students' disenchantment with their lecturers tended to subside over time. Merrill attributes this to the process of secondary socialisation; once the student has learned the ropes, she is able to cope with the variation in lecturer styles and perceived levels of competence. James refers to the shifting habitus of students, as they internalise the instrumentalist assumptions of higher education and organisational constraints under which lecturers work. The evidence of this research study of the first year experience was that the habitus of teachers was at odds with the assumptions and expectations of their students, especially during the first months. They then sought over time to accommodate themselves to the rules of the game, as defined by their teachers, even though they were often unclear as to what these rules were and what was their purpose.

If teaching was a fourth priority for university lecturers, then the personal tutorial role was even lower down the list. A number of the students in this study (ironically, those on a social work course, which arguably merits a high level of personal support) were not allocated personal tutors at all, and were expected to approach individual lecturers for support as and when they felt they needed it. Some found their tutors disinterested, even unhelpful; several decided that the time and money needed to travel to university for a personal tutorial was not worth it. Some participants preferred to separate their personal and educational lives, and had no wish to use tutorials to discuss their personal concerns (see also Edwards 1993). However, given the students' failure to comprehend academic language and the tasks assigned to them, it seems that the downgrading of tutorial support disadvantages students from non-traditional backgrounds. Personal tutorials could provide the opportunity to discuss and clarify what was required of them and support their efforts to hone their academic skills. In the event, they did neither of these effectively.

Cotterill and Waterhouse (1998), writing from a tutor perspective, relate the deskilling of the tutors' role to changes across the higher education sector as a whole. In particular, they point to the increased depersonalisation of the structure and purposes of higher education, as student numbers have grown without an increase in resources to support them. Technology has increasingly been seen as the answer to raising student intake at low cost, and New Right ideas around individual (as opposed to social) responsibility have become institutionalised. This depersonalisation, they argue, further disadvantages those who have historically been denied access to higher education and who are likely to need greater support than students from middle class backgrounds, who already know the rules of the higher education game. It also runs counter to a feminist view of academic relations, which might be characterised as supportive, reciprocal and humanised (Lather 1991). There are ways in which teacher habitus on the one hand, and the new environment of higher education on the other, work together to distance students from their teachers and tutors and to downgrade the pedagogic and supportive aspects of university learning. The onus is on the student to learn, to find her own way, or to give up the course.

Once in higher education, the students in this study faced difficulty in adjusting to its rules and norms, which were often tacit rather than explicit. Adjustment involved learning to write in a style and language appropriate to higher education. It was not simply a matter of spelling and grammar, but involved learning to subjugate their own substantial life experience to the experience of the academy. For students who had arrived at university by non A-Level routes, this was sometimes difficult. Access Courses, particularly those in the social sciences, had stressed the value of using their personal experience as material for discussion. Higher education did not. In trying to make the shift from using their own style of expression, participants sometimes seemed to over compensate by lifting large chunks of writing from books, rather than reading, paraphrasing and referencing authors' work, and ultimately becoming confused about what it was that their tutors required. The students were unwilling to seek clarification of confusing assignment tasks and blamed themselves for their failure to understand what was required of them. As relative novices, they found reading academic language difficult. They saw failure to understand as their own failure, rather than as a failure to communicate on the part of writers and academics. In doing so, they contributed to their own sense of exclusion from the world of high status learning. Once again, self-blame is a powerful force in perpetuating a sense of exclusion.

Widening participation whilst maintaining elitism

Social inclusion in education, widening participation and mass higher education are high on both governmental and institutional agendas. There is, however, a paradox. Although the number of non-traditional entrants to higher education has grown and the population of universities appears to be more diverse, there does not seem to have been a corresponding change in the extent to which non-traditional students experience university (particularly the traditional university) as inclusive. Debates continue within the academic world around quality versus quantity and the possible dumbing down of university education (Jary and Parker 1998). There is less discussion amongst policy makers about the purposes and methods of higher education, and the extent to which it serves the wider community as well as its own needs (Lave and Wenger 1991, Bowden and Marton 1998). University mission statements generally include reference to the advancement of learning through teaching, research and the dissemination of knowledge, and to the use of learning to benefit students and the wider community. However, universities also have a selective function; they serve to distribute social, cultural and, ultimately, economic capital. They are in the business of maintaining differentials, not creating equality. The activities and functions of higher education cannot be separated from the structural relations of the wider environment. And these relations involve inequalities, particularly economic inequalities.

One of the means by which these inequalities are maintained within higher education is through habitus. The habitus of universities, the curriculum and teachers, keeps the elitist university alive through the maintenance of well worn exclusionary practices and unquestioned traditions. The habitus of those labelled as non-standard or non-traditional tends to keep them away from higher status institutions and, if they do gain entry, tends to underline their sense of being outsiders.

Whilst it is not suggested that the exclusionary practices described in this chapter are necessarily deliberate or unchangeable, it does seem that they serve to retain certain prizes for a chosen few. High status qualifications are a product of their scarcity (Apple 1990). The more available a first degree becomes, the more its trade-in value varies, in accordance to where and how the degree was gained (Dore 1976). As more people have gained access to an undergraduate education, two trends have become apparent: the restratification of universities and the inflation of qualifications.

The change in the status of polytechnics since 1992 has not brought about unification in higher education. Rather, it has brought further stratification. In the eyes of potential students, as well as those already within higher education, there is a status divide between the pre- and post-1992 universities. This divide is apparent in the terms and conditions of teachers within the two types of university; it is seen in the relative value placed on teaching and research, and in the current obsession with league tables for almost every aspect of university activity. It is also visible in the resources available. Post-1992 universities are frequently housed on split sites, or cramped urban campuses, whereas the pre-1992 universities are likely to have extensive, purpose built and well resourced campuses. In this study it was manifested in the ways in which non-traditional students made university choices, based on their understanding of which students each type of institution is intended for. The traditional universities were seen as the preserve of the elite. Most of our students did not think they were intended for them; they were more likely to consign themselves to a post-1992 university. They knew their place.

As credential inflation continues, the second degree becomes the new benchmark. Access to study at postgraduate level, except in rare circumstances, is frequently dependent on the student either being able to pay her own fees or being sponsored by an employer. The working class student's relative lack of economic capital is likely to mean that she will remain excluded from higher level qualifications and hence greater economic rewards. And this effect is not just class-specific; Apple has also drawn attention to the impact of inflation qualification across class, race and gender lines in the United States' school system:

> In the past, as gains were made by ethnically different people, working class groups, women and others in schooling, one of the latent effects was to raise the credentials required by entire sectors of jobs. Thus race, class and gender barriers were partly maintained by an ever-increasing credential inflation. (Apple 1986, p. 167)

Increasingly, this seems to be the case in the UK higher education system. The government is in the process of introducing foundation degrees: two year, vocationally oriented, and employer led, a further stratum in the already stratified system. Foundation degrees are likely to be targeted at people from less wealthy socio-economic groups. The economic and social exchange rate of such degrees is likely to be lower than for full degrees. However, it will enable the claim for widening participation to be sustained, without altering the status and content of the traditional degree, nor requiring an institutional rethink of capital and habitus. It will be interesting to see who takes up these opportunities, which universities will promote them and how they will advance the interests of working class people, when it comes to reaping the economic rewards of a higher level education.

Is habitus all there is?

I began this study by listening to students talking about their experiences – of schooling, of careers advice, of college, of progress and setbacks. The study progressed through discussion about making choices, moving on, struggling to manage financially and getting to grips with university expectations. It culminated in public articulation of some of the institutional and environmental aspects of university life which persist in excluding working class and ethnic minority women from full participation and from being on equal terms with others. From this arose an analysis of why so little has changed, even amid the discourse of widening participation.

Both Bourdieu's analysis of habitus and capital, and Apple's analysis of exclusionary practices within educational institutions provide useful tools for exploring and explaining why institutional arrangements resist change. This is not however, to imply that the status quo is inevitable. Nor is it to imply that, for non-traditional students, there is nothing to be gained from higher education in terms of personal growth and learning. In many ways, old habitus can be overlaid by new, as when the student takes on aspects of the university habitus, a process sometimes referred to as socialisation or adjustment. Aspects of institutional practice may also change over time, and under pressure, both from outside and within. The questions which arise from this analysis are: how can the habitus of educational institutions be changed, how can the exclusionary practices which are perpetuated within universities be challenged and changed, how can the joint endeavours of students, teachers and researchers result in more than a mere redistribution of inequality? Is a radical change in the purposes and methods of higher education possible? The following chapters examine possible ways forward. Chapter ten identifies the paradoxes in national and institutional policy on higher education and suggests some of the institutional, policy and attitudinal changes which might make university a more relevant, and inclusive place. Chapter eleven draws out some of the lessons which Reachout learned from its own changing practice, which may be of use to other practitioners concerned with widening representation in higher education.

10

RESOLVING SOME PARADOXES

Yet how can something that seeks so fervently to help – as liberal educational theory and practice so clearly seek to do – be an ideological form that covers the reality of domination?
Michael Apple 1990, p. 20

They just want a certain kind of person . . . I think they just want to keep the status quo.
Salma: degree student

Five paradoxes

This chapter summarises some of the paradoxes of current national policy and institutional practice on widening participation and suggests areas where change is needed. It goes on to discuss how the diversity of non-traditional students' experience could be harnessed to promote learning, as well as improve the life chances of working class, black and Asian students, particularly those who have family responsibilities. There is evidence of a commitment (on paper, at any rate) to widening participation (Dearing 1997, Fryer 1997, DfEE 1998a, Blunkett 2000, Blackstone 2000, HEFCE 2001). Widening participation officers have been appointed in many UK universities, and there is no shortage of applications to the Higher Education Funding

Council of England for funding for widening participation initiatives. The evidence, however, still points to the fact that widening participation does not feel like a reality for some of those entering universities, particularly for mature students from non-traditional backgrounds. During the course of this research study, five paradoxes emerged which highlighted the difference between the rhetoric of widening participation and its reality. These paradoxes operated at both government and institutional levels.

Paradox one: widening participation, worsening finances

During the first five years since the Labour Government was elected, scarcely a week went by without reference in the media to the issue of equality in higher education. However, contradictions remain. As the widening participation agenda was trumpeted, a loan system for student maintenance was put in place. There is evidence that the current system of financing students has acted as a deterrent to university applications on the part of poorer people (Callender and Kemp 2000, Knowles 2000). There is no doubt that income and socio-economic status are still the main indicators of inequality in higher education (Dearing 1997). The evidence from this research is that financial hardship is a serious worry for prospective mature students from socio-economically disadvantaged backgrounds, and a serious problem for those who do take the risk of studying for a degree.

There has been one small but positive development in student funding. From October 1999, many students on part-time higher education courses, who are also on social security benefit or on low income, have been able to apply for fee waivers to enable them to meet some of the costs of part-time study. However, the situation for full-time students has not improved. The current government remains committed to a loan based funding system which involves students incurring large debts. The elite universities' response to this, and to their own cash constraints was to commission the controversial Greenaway Report (Greenaway and Haynes 2000), which recommended the introduction of increased top up fees, maintaining that this will benefit the socio-economically disadvantaged by releasing funds which can be used to offer bursaries for poorer students. At the time of writing, the issue remains unresolved, but there is every likelihood that such fees will eventually be imposed.

Far from widening participation, such a move is likely to have negative effects. The charging of differential fees is likely to further widen the status gap between universities, with the elite universities charging higher fees, and creating an impression that the education they offer is of higher quality and thus higher value. Furthermore, potential students from lower socio-economic groups are likely to be deterred by additional fees, whether or not bursaries are available. The process of applying for special financial support would create yet another bureaucratic barrier to poorer students applying to high charging universities, and reinforce their sense that such universities are not intended for students from low income backgrounds. To put the onus on poor students to come, cap in hand, for financial support is to take away their right to an education offered and provided on the basis of their ability to benefit from it, and to return some of these benefits to society.

The mechanisms of social exclusion are complex (Byrne 1999, Preece 1999) and it is quite possible for such mechanisms to operate within a context of inclusiveness. A combination of the present loan based system for financing student maintenance, and the prospect of the introduction of top up fees by some universities are indicators that it is possible to speak of widening access, whilst in reality, impeding it. The reintroduction of a grant, rather than a loan based system would ensure that those least able to cope with debt such as adults on low or benefit based incomes and those with family commitments – are able to contemplate higher education. The scrapping of notions such as top up fees would allow poorer students some choice in where to apply to university, rather than having their choice dictated by their ability to pay or their being prepared to beg for extra help.

Paradox two: higher qualifications, lower value

There is an assumption implicit in calls for increased participation in higher education that the more people who gain access to higher education, the more equitable the system will be. However, wider access does not necessarily mean greater equality. The government's policy for widening access has been directed towards promoting part-time higher education and, more recently, towards launching foundation degrees (already dubbed 'sub-degrees'), with their emphasis on short, vocational courses. Although the statistical illusion may be created that more people from lower socio-economic groups are entering higher education through such a route, the reality is that they are likely to be entering lower status higher education and leaving with lower status qualifications which reap smaller rewards. Students in this research were well aware of the differential value of certain qualifications and the variation in status between universities. It seems unlikely that the elite universities, many of which are happy to continue to recruit from their current constituency of 18 year old, middle class, A-Level students, will embrace these new qualifications. It is more likely that it will be left to the continuing education departments, the Open University and the post-1992 universities to develop them, thereby perpetuating status inequality between different types of institution and qualification.

It has been argued for a number of years both in the United Kingdom and elsewhere (Dore 1976, Bourdieu 1979, Apple 1986, Coffield and Williamson 1997) that an undergraduate degree or diploma no longer guarantees the financial and status rewards that it did, and that competition for credentials, alongside qualification inflation is forcing people to increase their levels of cultural capital by increasing the numbers and levels of qualifications they possess. A postgraduate qualification is therefore becoming increasingly important, whereas twenty years ago a first degree would have opened the door to improved prospects. At the same time, the availability of financial support for students wishing to undertake postgraduate study has decreased to a point where financial help is only accessible to the few, and post-graduate study frequently has to be financed by students themselves. It was certainly not accessible to the students in this study, who began and will end their undergraduate careers with family responsibilities, a burden of debt and an urgent need to find work as soon as possible. The creation of further layers of qualifications may increase the numbers gaining access to some kind of university qualification. Whether it will give them access to improved life chances is more questionable.

The continuing divide between research universities and teaching universities, between the Russell Group of elite universities and the rest, and between the vocational and the academic, does not serve the interests of people who have been traditionally under-represented in higher education. What is needed is parity of esteem and resources for universities and colleges of higher education, and alongside this, a clear pathway to qualifications which have value to the learner and enhance her competence and confidence in dealing with the range of problems and issues she will encounter in a working career.

Paradox three: access without accessibility

In spite of the financial difficulties and the uncertainty as to whether an undergraduate degree or diploma will really guarantee a better future, students in the Reachout project were putting their faith in the system, undertaking Access Courses and taking the risks involved in returning to study. With support and encouragement from Reachout, they were able to apply and gain access to higher education courses. However, the research into their experiences once they reached university revealed a gap between the rhetoric of access and the reality of day to day survival within institutions still geared to the needs of a different class of people: the child free, white, middle class, school leavers. This gap was particularly apparent in two areas of student experience: childcare and course arrangements.

Childcare arrangements

The research group and the students present at the *Students Speak* conference stressed the guilt felt by parents combining the demands of study and childcare, and the view that higher education institutions were poorly equipped to assist them. There was a feeling that students with children were unwelcome on higher education campuses and that their concerns about childcare were a purely personal matter. Where nursery provision was available, it was expensive and inflexible and did not take account of the women's need for after school care.

The attitude of universities towards students with children requires rethinking if they are serious about opening education to a wider range of learners. The tendency for universities to divorce themselves from the everyday demands of adult students' lives leads them to ignore students' childcare needs and to see their failure to manage the conflicting demands of home and study as their problem, rather than it being a legitimate issue. Children are integral to many mature students' lives. Indeed, most often, the students interviewed in the course of this study cited their children, and their concern for their future, as the reason for deciding to apply for university in the first place. The desire to provide positive role models for children and to ensure their financial future was very strong. Universities need to acknowledge this and to recognise that one of the ways they will make themselves more accessible to working class and ethnic minority people in future, is by enabling the future generation of students, the children of mature students, to feel that universities are welcoming sites of learning, not formidable, exclusive clubs for a small adult elite.

The problem of accessibility for parents with children is not only attitudinal, it is also financial. Students stressed the need for government to provide financial support for the attempts of parents to improve their prospects by aiming for higher education. The *Students Speak* conference recommended that assistance should be available towards the childcare costs of part time as well as full time students. This would involve providing finance for before and after school childcare, which gives parents time to study, as well as to attend lectures. Of the parents interviewed, all described their need to study late into the night, after their children were asleep, or in the early hours before they woke. Money was not available for parents who wished to use their free time in the holidays for study. Childcare arrangements were frequently precarious and dependent on the goodwill of relatives, because money was not available for registered nursery and after school provision. On site provision at universities, where it existed, was prohibitively expensive and inadequately subsidised. Whilst the government has shown itself prepared to finance the childcare costs of some mothers returning to short vocational courses via the New Deal for Lone Parents employment programme, it has only recently begun to recognise the needs of women wishing to enter higher education with the aim of securing a better long-term future for themselves (Blackstone 2000).

Childcare is expensive; good quality childcare is even more expensive. However, a commitment to wider participation has to be backed up by funding. If it is not, then it will be women – who still bear the major responsibility for childcare – and particularly lone mothers who will be penalised.

Course arrangements

Apart from the financial burden of childcare, the arrangement and timing of courses was difficult for parents attempting to combine study with childcare. The relatively short length of the university teaching year means that university courses involve an element of time serving. An undergraduate course, spread over three years and divided into three terms of ten or eleven weeks, is sustained only by the logic of tradition. Although it may be attractive to university academic staff, and to some students, who are able to enjoy the freedom of relatively long vacations, it does not suit non-traditional students for a number of reasons. From a financial point of view, it causes serious difficulty for poorer students, who are unable to claim benefit for the holiday period. Students who are also parents are rarely able to take up the option of working during the vacation, as the money they earn is used up in paying for the childcare necessary to go to work. Unlike their younger counterparts, they are rarely able to take the opportunity afforded by the long summer vacation either to work or to travel and refresh themselves. The staggering of full-time courses over three years, and part-time over six, affects older students both financially and in career terms. The older the student is when she graduates, the harder it will be for her to pay off her student loans and begin to feel the benefits of the increased potential earnings which higher education should bring. Students in their mid or late thirties were very concerned about the problem of debt, and were conscious that their chances of getting a job were likely to decrease with age (Purcell 2000). The university term system appears to be constructed for the benefit of the university's traditional constituency of students and its academic staff. It does not benefit poorer or older students.

There are two possible solutions to this problem, neither of which is mutually exclusive, but both of which are likely to be controversial. First, there is a need to introduce greater flexibility into the pace of student teaching and learning, a recommendation also supported by Preece (1999) in her study of community-based adult learning. Some universities, through making their courses modular, have improved this to a certain extent. However, if modularising courses is not accompanied by a commitment to choice and real flexibility in the timing and pace of study, its full potential benefits for students with complex life commitments will not be felt. Secondly, relatively minor increases in the length of university terms, such as tying them in with the current school terms, would increase the number of weeks a year that tutors were available to students. This would also mean an increase in the number of teachers and tutors available. It could decrease by at least one term the overall amount of time a student would need to spend at university in pursuit of a degree. Such changes, along with the improvements to childcare arrangements already suggested, might have some impact on the way in which students who are also parents feel that the universities are prepared to consider their needs, along with the needs of their traditional constituency of students without family responsibilities.

Paradox four: increasing support needs, decreasing support

Students from non-traditional backgrounds generally recognise their need to increase their academic knowledge and skills, and look to their university teachers and tutors to facilitate their learning. The experience of this study was that their expectation of receiving good guidance and support was often unfulfilled. In the first year they felt marginalised by their age, ethnicity, class or parental status, and unsupported. Although these feelings began to wane as they adjusted to the norms of university life (Merrill 1999) and grew to accept the situation (James 1998), there can be little doubt that their feelings of marginalisation made it more likely that they would leave the course early.

Students in this study had the support of Reachout throughout their university careers. A number of those interviewed spoke of the high drop-out rates from full-time courses among their fellow mature students who did not receive such support. For those on part-time, and particularly Open University courses, the sense of isolation was strongest. Unsurprisingly therefore, the early leaving rates of those who took part-time and distance learning courses were very high (a finding supported by McGivney, 1996). Studies of withdrawal rates from further and higher education courses concentrate on features of the students themselves – age, gender, previous qualifications, personal circumstances or on type of course and mode of study (Woodley *et al* 1987, McGivney 1996). Little research has been carried out to explore the role of the educational institutions in maintaining or impeding students' progress. Indeed, it is difficult to elicit students' reasons for leaving courses, owing to their tendency to blame themselves or their personal circumstances for their perceived failure (Preece 1999) and the difficulty in locating students who drop out. However, research participants frequently expressed disappointment at the lack of support they received. They felt they were expected to deal with their study or personal difficulties without bothering their tutors or teachers.

It is tempting for universities to blame students' drop-out on their failure to prepare themselves for or commit themselves to their studies. It is also tempting to conclude that widening participation means dumbing down – that the academic calibre of students is declining as mass higher education becomes a reality (Lucas and Webster 1998). However, there was considerable evidence in this study that although students from non-traditional backgrounds and their university teachers acknowledged the need for additional support, it was generally not forthcoming. If widening participation is to be made a reality, the nature of the relationship between the university and its students needs to change, and the habitus of teachers and tutors needs to shift.

One of the key features of an institution whose habitus is well established is that it does not need to explain its rules and norms. They are implicit and taken for granted. If universities are open, in the main, to the initiated, those whose educational, peer group and family connections have already passed on the rules of the game, it is unnecessary for the institution to make its norms explicit. However, if the university wishes to open its doors to the uninitiated, it must spell out what students can expect in terms of tutor support, lecturer quality and commitment, and also reveal the biases of its curriculum.

One of the problems in being explicit about aims, expectations and ethos is that it invites questions about the aims and methods of the university itself. Mature, experienced students, once they know the rules of the game, may well be likely to challenge them. This will be threatening to institutions as a whole, as well as to individual tutors, conscious of their own vulnerability, and under pressure from increasing management and inspectorial scrutiny (Cotterill and Waterhouse 1998). The fundamental basis of the relationship between students and their tutors is that it assumes that the tutor has knowledge and the student does not. Tutors who have worked within the higher education system for some time and who may feel relatively powerless in the face of the power of the university structure may, at the same time, be unaware of the power of their position. From the students' perspective, tutors distanced themselves from their concerns, seeing them as peripheral to the task of teaching and assessment, and avoided engagement with them. It was almost as if to engage with the realities of students' lives was to compromise their professionalism. What I would argue for is not a mawkish obsession with students' personal business, but for the development of relationships which are reciprocal and non-hierarchical, and which acknowledge that teachers, too, are learners and that they can learn from their students, as well as facilitate their learning.

Paradox five: changing knowledge, fixed curriculum

Mature students bring with them to university a wealth of experience gained from life and work. However, as has been noted elsewhere (Preece 1999), this experience is frequently undervalued by the institutions they enter and, in some cases, its expression is silenced. This was particularly the case for the black and Asian students in this study, who reported on the way in which discussions of their experiences of racism were 'swept under the table', rather than being used as the basis for the formation of knowledge and understanding about how racism operates.

The particular knowledge which marginalised people bring with them to the educational situation has been described as 'subjugated knowledge' (Foucault 1972). The exploration of subjugated knowledge can make a powerful challenge to dominant values (Preece 1999). Thus, it is perhaps not surprising that marginalised voices are silenced within the conservative atmosphere of higher education institutions. Preece has explored how university structures and personnel can operate to ensure that the potential of subjugated knowledge is stifled and that contesting existing views of knowledge can only be achieved through already accepted means:

> . . . University critical thinking takes place in a context which allows only certain view points, approved through authorised texts. New knowledge is allowed but only if it is derived in certain, approved ways – approved by those from within the system (primarily those who are white, male, able bodied and middle class). (Preece 1999, p. 5)

Thus, those who have been regarded as outsiders, marginalised by poverty and discrimination, are automatically denied a voice in redefining what it is that constitutes knowledge, how and by whom it should be taught, and how it should be assessed.

Participants in the *Students Speak* conference advocated more emphasis on forms of assessment which valued the skills and experience which mature students have gained outside the university such as their ability to speak up in class presentations and discussions, their community contacts and their interpersonal skills. Over the course of this research study, shifts have been discernible in some of their descriptions of their experiences of different teaching and assessment methods. For example, assessment tasks which involve class presentations and group discussion work have become more common and, in professional training, emphasis is now placed on students' ability to reflect on their practice. However, in the main, students' own experience was not seen as contributing to the development of knowledge. There is still a limit to the extent to which academia is prepared to link knowledge in practice with knowledge as theory.

Focusing on learning

During the latter part of this research, when I began to explore with students what they felt they had learned in their first year at university, there were indications that learning was taking place (although this was sometimes hard to discern beneath the expressions of financial despair, time pressure and personal isolation). Learning, as described by the participants and discussed in chapter six, was about increased self-knowledge and a broadening consciousness of the world outside their own lives. It was connected to placement practice, or to exposure to subject matter which was connected to their own lives and histories. What I eventually began to hear about learning was not about narrow subject knowledge or academic conventions but about something deeper, and more meaningful to them as individuals. Bowden and Marton (1998) have contrasted this 'deep' learning with the more 'surface' learning with its emphasis on text, recall of information and crude forms of assessment, which is, ironically, encouraged by the structure and processes of formal education:

> When children experience the requirements to learn, to achieve, to be clever and to show it to be the case by recalling, saying or doing something, there is a risk that the means (recalling, saying or doing

something) becomes an end in itself instead of the means that were supposed to indicate the outcomes (insights, capabilities, understanding). (Bowden and Marton 1998, p. 59)

From the evidence of this study, it seems that 'insights, capabilities and understanding' often became lost in the formal and more hidden demands of the higher education system. However, from the students' viewpoint, it was the realisation of the deep learning which was taking place which made their struggles worthwhile.

A number of researchers (Lave and Wenger 1991, Bowden and Marton 1998) are making the case, from within the higher education institutions themselves, for a redefinition of the aims, purposes and methods of higher education. From the United States, Lave and Wenger (1991) make a powerful argument for a new type of learning, which takes into account the whole person and combines both practical skill and academic knowledge, without prioritising one over the other. From Australia and Sweden, Bowden and Marton (1998) envisage a 'university of learning', in which teaching, learning and service to the community are the combined aims of education, in contrast to the increasingly compartmentalised notions of teaching and research. Such a university would, they argue, be aimed at knowledge formation and preparing students for effective action in future situations as yet unknown. If this were the case, the knowledge and experience which mature, working class, black and Asian students bring with them would be seen a welcome asset to the university's knowledge store. They, in turn, could gain skills and confidence in analysis and problem solving which would enhance their ability to operate in the complex and demanding world of work. But instead, they are in danger of working for ever-devaluing certificates testifying to their ability to recall a narrow range of unwanted facts. In the United Kingdom, McNair (1997), Preece (1999) and others are calling for a democratisation of the purposes, processes and outcomes of higher education. As yet, there is little sign that these voices are being heard.

What hope then, is there for the marginalised and silenced students? And what hope for one community based worker and researcher in a small, short term funded project? The following chapter puts forward some of the lessons for practice which have been indicated through the process of the research.

11

SOME LESSONS FROM PRACTICE

We must shift the role of critical intellectuals from being uni-versalising spokespersons to acting as cultural workers whose task is to take away the barriers that prevent people from speaking for themselves.

Michael Apple 1991, p. ix

This chapter summarises some of the lessons learned during the course of the past four years' work and research. This research study began as an evaluation of Reachout, a small scale, community based educational project, funded by a short term government initiative. One of the arguments frequently advanced to me against the mainstreaming of widening participation initiatives, is that in these times of financial stringency in higher education, it is too expensive. So it is worth briefly highlighting some of the achievements of Reachout, in the light of the investment of public money involved. £280,000 was originally made available by the Government to run the project for three and a half years. A budget of around £80,000 a year therefore covered the cost of a full-time worker, a part-time administrator and a small team of part-time tutors, as well as office costs, course materials, child-care, an access course, residential weekends and day courses. Over its three and a half year funding period, the project offered educational advice and support to almost 650 people. 133 of these people eventually entered full or part-time higher education with Reachout's support. A further 149 entered further education, vocational training, job opportunities or voluntary work.

If progress to higher education alone were to be the criterion of Reachout's success and cost effectiveness, this was achieved at an average cost of around £2,000 per student. This compares well to the estimated teaching costs of £4,790 (Greenaway and Haynes 2000) per student for three year's study at university, and a minimum cost to the government of £12,000 in loans and hardship grants for student maintenance. Against these crude quantitative measures Reachout's performance provided value for money.

The project was also able to unlock other financial resources for its participants, including securing charitable funds for course fees, books and childcare, and donations of computers which had been discarded as out of date by university departments. Thus, a further thirty people were helped in concrete ways to maintain themselves in higher education. This had an important impact on a number of students who felt that, without such support, they would have been unable to contemplate returning to study. One of the lessons learned, therefore, was that it is possible for a relatively small financial investment to offer tangible and quantifiable benefits for students from non-traditional backgrounds.

However the course of the research has raised issues with implications beyond the purely financial. There have also been lessons about the quality and nature of work aimed at widening participation. I present below some of the practical lessons from Reachout's intervention, and some of the principles which have grown out of the process of action research that have been important in ensuring the successful educational progress of many of Reachout's students.

Practical lessons

It has been noted (Preece 1999) that community-based staff in higher education often enjoy 'autonomy without authoritative status'. Whilst it is possible, operating from outside the educational institution, to bring about change for individual students, it is difficult to get universities to respond to the demands which emerge from community based work.

Community-based education workers are often outsiders in their own institution (Preece 1999, Bellis *et al* 1999).

My own experience is that there is certainly some truth in their assertion that community-based staff are marginalised and powerless and that because of their physical separation from the university campus, their funding is liable to be limited or short term. However, the combined role of community-based education worker and researcher does allow certain room for manoeuvre. An action research role offers the community based worker credibility in the eyes of higher education institutions; it enables her to communicate effectively through the use of academic language, academic conferences, and through the publication of academic articles and papers. Whilst this may not bring about major changes in practice and policy, it may stimulate changes in attitude amongst those who wish to listen.

There are, however, a number of ways in which an action research approach may have enabled Reachout students to enjoy a more positive experience of higher education than might otherwise have been the case. The lessons of Reachout's experience and of the involvement of its students in the research process, has allowed some principles to be developed in practice. In arguing for practical measures to promote equality, Lynch (1999, p. 291), has made a distinction between enabling and encouraging participation. Reachout's ability to enable participation was limited by its resources. It was recognised early on that there were obvious material barriers to adults wishing to return to study. The major obstacles, as mentioned above, were finance and childcare costs. As well as attracting and disbursing financial help for its students, Reachout was active in highlighting and publicising the financial difficulties faced by mature students who were parents. As well as enabling participation through the provision of courses, advice and information, Reachout was also successful in encouraging participation. In doing so, it developed some guiding principles which, in practice, helped to motivate students to take steps towards higher education and sustained them while they were there.

Guiding principles
Feedback from our project students indicated that there were particular features of Reachout's work which made it accessible and supportive in

ways not experienced with other forms of educational provision. The project attempted to build a bridge between its students and higher education, whilst also creating a safety net, which could support them if they faltered in their progress, or if they were unable to find support within the university itself, or from their family or peers. There were three distinct elements to the encouragement provided:

- demystifying academia

- building support networks

- breaking down hierarchies

Demystifying academia

There was a tendency, noted in earlier chapters, for non-traditional students to blame themselves for not understanding the norms of university study. Participants often cast themselves as inadequate and unworthy, because they had not arrived at university by the traditionally accepted, A-Level route. They would therefore describe themselves negatively as learners, rather than positively as people with considerable insight, based on their wide experience of life and work. They wanted to know 'what they [the tutors] want'. An important aspect of Reachout's work was therefore to demystify the world of academia. This entailed preparing students for the demands of university study, particularly the demands of assessment via essays, and encouraging university teachers to speak directly to them about what they could expect when they entered university.

Reachout organised preparation for higher education courses which involved students in looking at and assessing past essays of other students – something they had never done before, essay writing being such a private activity. In doing this, they had access to the marking criteria used by local universities and gained insight into the assessment priorities of essay markers. This enabled discussion on essay structuring, academic language and conventions, and marking levels. It also revealed inconsistencies in markers' preferences and expectations, as well as the fact that assessment tasks were sometimes ambiguous and confusing. This led participants into discussion of how to approach tutors, ask questions and speak up when they were uncertain or unhappy about assessment tasks. This may have encouraged students to shift responsibility from themselves for knowing what tutors wanted, and to expect their tutors to take responsibility for clarifying tasks.

University teachers were by no means entirely unapproachable, and in each of the higher education institutions with which Reachout worked, there were sympathetic, helpful and committed teachers, who were keen to come and meet students, answer their questions about university study, and give them a realistic sense of what support they might expect in their studies. Some lecturers also invited students to come to the university and see for themselves what the environment was like. Generally, the Reachout students were surprised at the lack of tutorial support they would be offered, having expected that it would be more frequent and intensive. However, this knowledge provided them with the incentive to build up alternative support networks among their peers and in their community, which would be necessary to sustain them through two or three years of study.

Building support networks

A crucial principle of Reachout's development was that it began and remained rooted in its community. Although participants were encouraged to visit universities before applying and to attend courses to prepare themselves for the expectations of university life, it was recognised that mature students with family and community responsibilities needed support within their localities. Reachout's presence in the locality, rather than in the institution, made it more sensitive to local needs and helped it to:

> . . . create close links with the community and listen to what they are saying about the institutional obstacles that are experienced. (Burton 1993, p. 287)

In her discussion of race and gender in educational management, Burton (1993) stresses the importance of support networks in fostering solidarity amongst those who may be marginalised or relatively powerless. Students in this study often expressed a sense of isolation brought about by their poverty, ethnicity, age or lone parent status. It was important that such networks were based in the communities in which they lived. The amount of time students were able to spend at the university itself was limited by childcare, family and work commitments. They were therefore unable to take full advantage of the formal support services provided on campus: students' unions, counselling and study support services, or the more informal support of colleagues, which is often found outside the lecture room, in the bars and canteens of the university.

Reachout encouraged the establishment of support networks by consciously fostering supportive links between its students throughout their progress through higher education. This was achieved in part through preparation weekends and group sessions designed to focus on common concerns about going to university: childcare, finance and study skills. These sessions built a sense of common cause among them and helped them to get to know of others in their locality who would be in a similar position. By providing drop-in study support facilities at local libraries and community centres, Reachout offered students help outside the university setting from tutors who were there not to judge or assess their efforts but to act as critical friends, offering suggestions about their work, providing a sounding board for academic ideas and encouraging students when they were feeling uncertain or unconfident.

Finally, as participants began to move through their university careers, they in turn were encouraged to support others who were just beginning. Burton (1993) also stresses the importance of significant people in nurturing the career development of women and of those from ethnic minorities. Students in this study frequently mentioned individuals who had been significant in encouraging them to make educational progress. Unlike Burton's interviewees, however, Reachout students tended not to mention family members as key people in this respect, as they felt that their parents lacked access to educational information and networks. They were more likely to mention chance encounters with supportive individuals or professionals who had advised and encouraged them. The project attempted to replicate this role within the community by providing educational advice sessions at local community venues, by following up advice with sustained support and encouragement and by helping them access information and develop skills to achieve their goals.

As the project progressed, Reachout students themselves began to take on a supportive role within their localities, talking to other parents at the school gates, at church or in the doctor's surgery. They were able to give advice and encouragement from their own experience, as well as to refer people for help. In this way a network of support began to develop, which cut across boundaries of subject, course and institution, and which was not dependent on either Reachout or any other educational agency. An informal system of support had been created, which involved the development of peer group friendship, guidance and advice but was not complicated by any element of supervision or assessment. Later, training was offered to students who had graduated from university to help them develop their skills as mentors in supporting less confident students who are beginning their university careers. Finally, as the first former Reachout students have graduated and moved into employment in education, community work and social work, they have been able to offer the benefit of their experiences, this time in a professional capacity.

Breaking down hierarchies

Lynch (1999, p. 303) has argued that if educational structures and practices are not participatory, the hidden curriculum of dominance and inequality will eclipse formal commitments to equality. Student-teacher relationships reflect the disparity in power between learner and teacher. The idea of professional distance features strongly in the way university teachers interpret their role. The research participants wanted the student–teacher relationship to be one of power sharing and mutual respect. This was rarely felt to be the case in higher education, and disillusionment was expressed at the distance which tutors placed between themselves and their students, and at their inaccessibility.

As Reachout's work developed, it became evident that participants benefited from an approach which was reciprocal, and which acknowledged their existence as whole people, with personal concerns and individual expertise. This became fundamental to the way in which the project operated, and was brought about by a conscious attempt to break down the usual hierarchical relationship between expert staff and inexpert student. The project tried to develop pedagogical and organisational styles which operated against the development of hierarchies. The teaching materials used were designed to build on students' personal and life experiences, and to help them to develop academic skills through the articulation of these experiences. The design, content and timing of courses were based on their expression of need, rather than on the basis of the decisions of academic committees or the requirements of accrediting bodies. Thus, courses on financing higher education and preparing for university study were organised specifically in response to students' requests, as was the development of study retreats, which enabled students to have a day of private study, with childcare, lunch and tutor support provided, if required.

An open door policy was established within the community-based project office, where further and higher education students could come to study, seek advice and build social networks. Open access to support and guidance broke down the distinction between expert and novice. Students in such a setting were often able to offer advice and support to other students, when staff were unable to do so. For example, in the complex area of study and the benefit system, the students themselves were more expert at advising their contemporaries than the project staff. They were the people who had recent and first hand knowledge of the problems of finance and study. On an academic level, an open door policy meant that staff were able to encourage students to share knowledge, information and learning resources, and could link students together, helping them to form networks which would sustain them through their studies. Ultimately, this benefited not only the students, but also Reachout.

An open access office, where staff and students mingled, meant that information about the project, its funding and its dynamics was freely shared between staff and students. Confidentiality was limited to students' personal matters. Thus, those who regularly used Reachout as a support, automatically knew what its problems and successes were. At a time of funding uncertainty (from 1998 to late 1999) this knowledge meant that they were both willing and able to lend support to efforts to keep the project going, as well as providing personal support to its staff. They were prepared to contact members of parliament and local councillors, to talk to charitable trusts, to speak at conferences and meetings and to show evidence of the usefulness of the project in ensuring their success. Their efforts contributed in large measure to the re-funding of the project for a further three years when its initial grant expired. The breaking down of professional hierarchies brought benefits to the project, as well as its students, and arguably ensured its survival.

Working for change

The fact that, in 1999, Reachout secured this further three years funding from the Higher Education Funding Council for England's widening participation initiative suggests that, for whatever political, economic or social reason, the government remains committed to increasing the proportion of people from lower socio-economic groups who enter higher education. Their interest is now focused on eighteen to twenty-one year olds, rather than those who, having experienced past exclusion, work and family commitments, have much to offer a university which is committed to diversity. There have been policy changes which suggest that the political will exists to offer further financial support to full-time higher education students who are parents. From September 2001, full-time higher education students who are also parents are entitled to some government support to help with their childcare costs during term time. Thus, for the mature student who is also a parent, it has become a little easier to contemplate university entry. Financial barriers remain: the university loan system is still in place and substantial debt is still a reality. However, university-level qualifications are still seen by Reachout students as a way of escaping the trap of poverty, low pay and low social status. What is less clear is whether the institutions of higher education, and those who define and validate what is thought to be desirable knowledge, share the commitment to changing themselves and their inbuilt exclusionary practices. There is some evidence that, for the elite universities at any rate, widening participation takes second place to a prestigious research reputation and to attracting students with standard A-Level grades, who are likely to be able to fit within the traditional university structures and norms with minimal support.

The final chapter of this book presents Salma's critical view of the current state of higher education and of her own prospects as a graduate. It also highlights one of the issues that have yet to be addressed through research and action aimed at creating equality in higher education: will the experience of a university education for working class, ethnic minority adults reap rewards in terms of better career and pay prospects and a better life for the future generation?

12

POSTSCRIPT:
DISCUSSION WITH SALMA

Salma was the first Reachout student to enter full time higher education. We kept in touch throughout her three years at university. Salma graduated in the summer of 2000. She gained a lower second degree in social policy. This discussion (which has been slightly abridged) took place a few days after Salma received her final results. The transcript was checked and approved by Salma.

MB: When I first interviewed you, there was a real sort of 'culture shock' about going to university. I got a really strong sense of alienation. And that hit me really hard. Because I thought, once our students got to higher education that would be fine. And it clearly wasn't. So what I'm interested in is how that developed, and whether your really strong feelings of marginalisation that you felt then carried on. And to talk through how you feel about university now.

S: Well, I think at first it was really difficult. It wasn't just the culture shock; it was due to the change in my lifestyle, the children's lives as well. That was really difficult. Rearranging our life to cope with studies. And throughout, the children came first. I had to give them quality time.

I've always really worked after they've gone to bed. So that was really hard because when they'd gone to bed, I was tired myself. I just had to force myself to do the reading and essay writing, just to keep my head above water.

MB: So – did it get easier?

S: I think the feeling of marginalisation got easier. I think you get accustomed to the environment and don't feel as marginalised.

MB: Did it change to accommodate you at all?

S: I think I perhaps changed. I don't think they did!

MB: I remember really vividly you saying that you'd gone to tutors when the financial situation was really difficult and it looked like your fees wouldn't be paid. The kind of response you got from tutors was really unsupportive.

S: Yes: 'Sort it out or you're going to be kicked out.' My personal tutor asked how it was going – this was my first term. And I explained that it was really, really difficult. And he turned round and said: It's difficult for the younger students as well because they go out to night clubs. And that shocked me really. I thought, don't talk about your problems to tutors. Keep them to yourself.

MB: And is that what you did in the end?

S: Basically, yes. I was shocked by what he said. It was like: you've got no right to complain. I could have said, well, they go night clubbing out of choice. They have a choice, I haven't.

MB: But you didn't?

S: No. I think I would have in my third year or second year. In your first year, you just don't have the confidence. It's such a strange environment. In such a major, white, middle class institution. You're so out of it, you feel as if you haven't got the right, and if you do say something they won't listen.

MB: So, how did you get through it? How did you manage it? Did you just keep it all to yourself?

S: Yes I did. We sort of discussed this at the conference. When mature students go into higher education, even members of the family think they've changed. I think there's a bit of envy involved as well. You can't really talk to them. Mum and Dad wouldn't really understand what was happening. You just have to get on with it. So I really had no one to talk to. And I didn't want to give up.

MB: You were always determined that you wouldn't.

S: For the children's sake, probably. It's a case of 'practice what you preach'. I'd love them to go into education. I want them to be successful. I think more so because they're girls. It's harder if you are a girl. So I thought – show by example.

MB: So, in a sense, a lot of it has been about them really, hasn't it?

S: Yes. And also being a lone parent, I've always been aware of the stigma attached to being a lone parent. And I didn't want to be on state benefit. There's a stigma attached to that as well. You can't really provide a decent life for your children and for yourself if you're just living hand to mouth, on social security. And I think the only way you can get out of that situation is by having a decent education. And more so if you're black, a minority woman.

MB: The other thing that really struck me when we spoke before was the contrast you made – and I've actually used it when I've written, because it was really powerful – between the subject matter, and your experience. And you said: they talk about people like me in social policy – in an academic way, without being sensitive to your actual lived experience. Did you feel that all the way through?

S: I think it cropped up in most of the modules. In Health – how ethnic minorities are marginalised in the NHS; Poverty and Social Security – how they don't receive the same treatment as white people, or even the same amount of help. Everything really. And they were talking about the most marginalised, the most poverty stricken people who are lone parents, and then it's like Pakistanis and Bangladeshis, living in private rented accommodation, in the inner city. They were basically talking about people like me.

MB: How did you feel about that? Did you ever feel able to speak about that?

S: No. In such an environment, you don't want to admit to being poor. I remember one of the professors talking about constitutional changes – changes to the House of Lords. And he said: That's not going to affect people who come from Aston – one of the poorest wards in north Birmingham. I don't think for one moment that he envisaged that there might be a student present who actually came from Aston. I live in Aston. But I think that they think that there's nobody who comes from an inner city deprived area when they're talking about this. It's just in abstract terms. And I don't think most of the other students would realise that there was someone who was at their university living in those circumstances.

MB: One of the things that came out of my research as a whole, and I was interested in your views on this, is the way that a lot of students, particularly black and Asian students, talk about their experience as being 'silenced'. That there are certain areas that don't get talked about, particularly around 'race', but also around poverty and class. Did you feel that your experience was silenced? You say you just never said anything, you just kept it separate.

S: I think they did talk about 'race'. But if you look at it – there were around twelve lectures a term, and if there was something on 'race', it would be the last lecture. Always. I don't know why. The last lecture in the module would be on 'race'. Just before we would break up. And sometimes people don't turn up at the last lecture. It's too close to the holidays. And it was a white student friend who pointed it out to me. I wonder why issues around 'race' get left to last?.

MB: That's funny, because other people have said that: they always raise the issue at the end of the session.

S: Yes. As if it's not important. They just shove it at the end. It was like that in the Housing module, and in the Health module. It was the last session.

MB: That's what's really surprised me. It's not that there would necessarily be overt racism, just this pushing it to the side and making it not controversial. By putting it at the end, or dealing with it right at the end of the session. That really struck me. So, you really seem to be saying that what you did was separate out your life from what you talked about in studying.

S: Yes.

MB: Do you think you had a valuable learning experience?

S: Yes, I do. It's opened my eyes up to a lot more subjects. For instance, politics. Well, I've always been interested, but I wasn't aware of different kinds of socialism and conservatism. I didn't particularly enjoy it, but I understand a lot more of it. I mean, obviously if you do a module, you get a deeper understanding. It widens your horizons, you question things. Whereas before the degree I perhaps would have seen something and not questioned it so much. Now you read more into it than meets the eye. You look into it deeper.

MB: Has that changed your life in any way, outside university? Does it make a difference to how you live your life?

S: Not really. I can't see how it does.

MB: I was just wondering, I suppose, if you're more aware of politics in the world around you, does it make you more active or less active or has it changed the way you deal with things?

S: It changed my way of being able to voice my views more. Whereas before I would have just stayed quiet, I'd say nothing.

MB: But you didn't feel able to do that at university? That's the funny thing isn't it?

S: I think it's being part of being an ethnic minority. You're one on your own. And there were a couple of other ethnic minorities, not in my particular course. But they were from well off backgrounds, middle class backgrounds.

MB: So did you always feel an outsider in a sense all the way through?

S: I suppose I did feel that less in the third year. I had gained more confidence. But you do feel like an outsider, and when you think about it, you are. I suppose you feel it more because of the type of institution it is. Middle class and white.

MB: The other thing we talked about that last time we met was – should you have chosen another university, that was maybe a bit more mixed, or that you may have felt more comfortable in. How do you feel about that now?

S: I feel fine with it now.

MB: You feel you made the right choice?

S: Yes. It's taken three years! But if somebody was in the same position as me, I wouldn't advise them to do it. I found the atmosphere intimidating when I first went to university. Of course, I haven't got any experience of any other university to compare it with. But my youngest sister, who is also a student, visited a number of universities and found that she felt uncomfortable and out of place at Brookvale.

I'm just thinking about the first year. How I felt. I wouldn't want them to drop out. I think I'm a fairly strong person and I didn't want to quit. But maybe another person might not be as strong. And I wouldn't want them to drop out. My concern is particularly about ethnic minority lone parents who have more than enough stresses to cope with anyway.

MB: We talked a lot too, about the financial side of studying. Let's talk about how that worked out in the end. Did you manage?

S: I think I managed. I only kept my head above water because I took out loans. I didn't want to take out loans, but I had to. I took out a student loan in the second year. Only because at the time, I didn't have any choice. But I wasn't comfortable with it. I hate the idea of debt.

MB: At the point when I interviewed you before, you had no money at all, in effect. Because they cut off your benefit, and you hadn't got your loan.

S: Yes, the first semester was terrible. Because I was told by the advisor that I was fine, because I was a lone parent. I could go into higher education. Little did he know. Because I don't think that very many people who are on social security go into higher education, so the advisors don't know anything about it.

MB: I remember, I was so horrified that you had basically nothing to live on at that point.

S: Yes. It was horrible. It was a nightmare!

MB: So, financially, would you advise people to – if you knew somebody else in your situation, what would you advise them?

S: Well, I know that at the conference it came out that perhaps they should be paid weekly. I think if they can budget wisely and they know they can, then I think they can make ends meet and with help from Reachout. If you've got a family that's helping you, and childcare costs are being met, then I suppose it's the same sort of financial situation as being on social security. It's roughly the same. But you just have to put it by.

MB: So you managed in the end?

S: Yes, in that sense. But I only buy the children's clothes, on the whole, in the sales. I'm a bargain hunter. I've had to be. And my parents have been really good. They've been supportive like that. So I think that helps. If you've got family support as well. But when all is said and done, I've been worse off being a student.

I think, if you take out your family support, take out the support you get from Reachout, there's no way you could cope.

MB: You've got to have other support?

S: Yes. You just dig a big hole by taking out more loans.

MB: Yes. You didn't take a bank loan?

S: No. I'd never do that.

MB: So, what do you think you've learned? What has the last three years taught you that you could maybe pass on to other people?

S: It's taught me to manage my time. Time management. I think it's taught me how to cope with stress. I've not coped very well, but I think the last three years, I've been under quite a lot of stress. And if you can do that, and give time to your children – to enable them to grow up as good people, and to help them with their work. As I said, it's taught me to analyse things, to question things. And it's given me the confidence as well, to speak out. And I think it's raised my self-esteem as well.

MB: You've mentioned the conference once or twice. Did you think that was valuable for mature students, or do you think it was a waste of time?

S: Yes, I think it was really valuable. Because it gave us a voice. And the lecturers had to sit there and take on board and listen to what we were saying. I don't think they understood the problems mature students experience. Moreover, it helped me personally, because it revealed that other students felt the same way as I did. Problems were discussed and shared.

MB: I'd be interested to know if they did – listen.

S: They were listening. I felt they were listening.

MB: And did you feel able to tell them what your experiences were?

S: I think most of the students did voice their experiences. I did most of the time, some of them were quite vocal.

MB: People have been very struck. When I've used some of the bits from interviews.

S: I think it has made a difference. At the start of my third year, a letter got sent to mature students. That really did make a difference. A lecturer made himself known as the mature students liaison officer, and that if there were any problems for mature students, he was there. The fact that he took it on board, I think it was due to the conference. And he wrote to us at the beginning of the semester, whereas there was no such letter at the beginning of the first or second year. I think it was as a result of him being at the conference and taking on board what was being said.

MB: I think what I wanted was that students did feel that, for once, they could have a voice on equal terms. And say – this is how we feel. I think I was disappointed that there weren't masses of changes. But I think I was being naive. I thought everything would change. But maybe they're small changes.

S: Yes, I think that was a very small change, but it would have an effect on a first year student. The consequence of them seeing that particular lecturer that at least they know that there's someone they can turn to.

MB: I hope so. As I've used bits of our transcripts and stuff, it's been really interesting talking to groups of lecturers about the issues. I did one the other week, I did a seminar on the issue and people are still shocked. They find it hard to believe that students have the experiences that we were saying. They found it hard to believe.

S: Because they're white and middle class. And they have no experience.

MB: They were. I've also spoken to a group of mature students, and their lecturers were there as well. And the mature students said that's exactly how we feel.

MB: So what about the future then? What do you hope?

S: I want to find a job soon.

MB: Have you got worries about that?

S: I have, yes. I did a module on gerontology. There's so much ageism out there. It's not really talked about. We talk about sexism, and we talk about racism and it's been quite well documented that if you're a mature student, I think you're three times less likely to find a job. If you're a minority it's harder again; if you're a woman, it's harder still. So it's like a triple jeopardy thing.

Not having enough work experience as well counts against you. I'm not stressing myself out too much at the moment. I think I've slowly become an optimist. After three years, you have to be! You have to believe in yourself, and believe that things are going to turn out for the best.

Salma was unemployed for over a year after graduating. She eventually found work as a further education lecturer.

BIBLIOGRAPHY

Adams, Robert (1993) *Quality Social Work* Basingstoke: Macmillan

Apple, Michael (1986) *Teachers and Texts: a political economy of class and gender relations in education.* London: Routledge and Kegan Paul

Apple, Michael (1990) *Ideology and Curriculum* London: Routledge

Apple, Michael (1991) 'Series Editor's Introduction' in Lather, Patti *Getting Smart: Feminist research and pedagogy with/in the postmodern* London: Routledge

Apple, Michael (1993) *Official Knowledge* London: Routledge

Arnot, Madeleine and Weiner, Gaby (eds) (1987) *Gender and the Politics of Schooling* London: Open University

Atweh, Bill, Kemmis, Stephen and Weeks, Patricia (1998) *Action Research in Practice: Partnerships for Social Justice in Education* London: Routledge

Barnes, Marian and Warren, Lorna (eds) (1999) *Paths to Empowerment* Bristol: The Policy Press

Belenky, Mary, Clinchy, Blythe, Goldberger, Nancy and Tarule, Jill (1986) *Women's Ways of Knowing: The Development of Self, Voice and Mind* New York: Basic Books

Bellis, Anne, Clarke, Jane, Ward, Jill (1999) *Marginalised Voices: A survey of current practice in widening participation with minority ethnic communities* Cambridge: Universities Association for Continuing Education

Bernstein, Basil (1973) *Class Codes and Control*, Vol. 1, *Theoretical Studies Towards a Sociology of Language* London: Paladin

Bhavnani, Kum-Kum. (1988) 'Empowerment and Social Research'. *Text* Vol. 8, Nos. 1–2, pp. 41–50

Bhavnani, Kum-Kum (1994) 'Shifting Identities, Shifting Racisms', *Feminism and Psychology* Vol. 4, No. 1, pp. 5–18

Blackstone, Tessa: Keynote Speech to CVCP Conference: *Mature Students: encouraging participation and achievement* 10th October 2000

181

Blunkett, David (2000) 'Reaching Out to Make Society Just', *Times Higher Education Supplement* 12th May 2000

Bourdieu, Pierre (1966) 'Intellectual Field and Creative Project', in Young, Michael (ed) (1971) *Knowledge and Control: New directions for the Sociology of Education* London: Collier Macmillan

Bourdieu, Pierre (1977) *Outline of a Theory of Practice* Cambridge: Cambridge University Press

Bourdieu, Pierre (1979) *The Inheritors: French Students and their relation to culture* London: University of Chicago Press

Bourdieu, Pierre (1997) 'The Forms of Capital' in Halsey, A. H., Lauder, Hugh, Brown, Phillip and Stuart Wells, Amy *Education: Culture, Economy, Society* Oxford: Oxford University Press

Bourdieu, Pierre and Passeron, Jean-Claude (1977) *Reproduction in Education, Society and Culture* London: Sage

Bourgeois, Etienne, Duke, Chris, Luc-Gyot, Jean and Merrill, Barbara (1999) *The Adult University* Buckingham: SRHE/ Open University Press

Bowden, John and Marton, Ference (1998) *The University of Learning: Beyond quality and competence in higher education* London: Kogan Page

Bowl, Marion (1998) *Experiencing the Barriers. Birmingham REACHOUT: A flexible approach to adult access to higher education.* Birmingham REACHOUT

Bowles, Samuel and Gintis, Herbert (1976) *Schooling in Capitalist America* London: Routledge and Kegan Paul

Brown, Phillip (1987) *Schooling Ordinary Kids* London: Tavistock

Burke, Penny, J. (2002) *Accessing Education: effectively widening participation* Stoke on Trent: Trentham Books

Burton, Leone (1993) 'Management, 'Race' and Gender: an unlikely alliance?' *British Educational Research Journal* Vol.19, No. 3, pp. 275–290

Byrne, David (1999) *Social Exclusion* Buckingham: Open University Press

Calder, Judith (ed) (1993) *Disaffection and Diversity: Overcoming Barriers for Adult Learners* London: Falmer Press

Callender, Claire and Kemp, Martin (2000) *Changing Student Finances: Income, Expenditure and the Take-up of Student Loans Among Full- and Part-time Higher Education Students in 1998/9* Nottingham: DfEE Publications

Carr, Wilf and Kemmis, Stephen (1986) *Becoming Critical: Education, Knowledge and Action Research* London: Falmer Press

CCETSW (1991) *Paper 30: Rules and Requirements for the Diploma in Social Work.* (2nd edn) London: CCETSW

Coffield, Frank and Williamson, Bill (1997) *Repositioning Higher Education* Buckingham: SRHE/ Open University Press

Collins, Patricia Hill (1991) *Black Feminist Thought: Knowledge, Consciousness and the Politics of Empowerment* London: Routledge

Cotterill, Pamela and Waterhouse, Ruth L (1998) 'Speaking Confidentially, or How Long Have I Got? The Demise of the Personal Tutorial in Higher Education' in Jary, David and Parker, Martin. *The New Higher Education: Issues and Directions for the Post-Dearing University* Stoke on Trent: Staffordshire University Press

Cross, Patricia (1981) *Adults as Learners* San Francisco: Jossey-Bass

Davies, Sue, Lubelska, Cathy and Quinn, Jocey (eds.) (1994) *Changing the Subject: Women in Higher Education* London: Taylor and Francis

Dearing, Sir Ron (1997) *Higher Education in the Learning Society* London: National Committee of Inquiry into Higher Education

Delamont, Sara (1980) *Sex Roles and the School* London: Routledge

DfEE (1998a) *The Learning Age: a renaissance for a new Britain* London: HMSO

DfEE (1998b) *Financial Support for Mature Students in Higher Education in 1998/99* London: Department for Education and Employment

DfEE (1999) *Learning to Succeed* London: HMSO

Dominelli, Lena (1988) *Anti-racist Social Work* Basingstoke: Macmillan

Dore, Ron (1976) *The Diploma Disease.* Lavenham: George Allen and Unwin

Edwards, Janice (1994) *The Scars of Dyslexia* London: Cassell

Edwards, Rosalind (1993) *Mature Women Students: Separating or Connecting Family and Education* London: Taylor and Francis

Foucault, Michel (1972) *The Archaeology of Knowledge* London: Routledge

Fryer, Robert (1997) *Learning for the Twenty-first Century: First Report of the National Advisory Group for Continuing Education and Lifelong Learning* London: NAGCELL

Gaster, Lucy (2002) *Past it at 40?: A grassroots view of ageism and discrimination in employment* Bristol: Policy Press

Gilligan, Carol (1982) *In a Different Voice* Cambridge: Harvard University Press

Glover, Ian and Branine, Mohamed (2001) *Ageism in Work and Employment* Aldershot: Ashgate

Gorard, Stephen, Selwyn, Neil and Williams, Sarah (2000) 'Must Try Harder! Problems Facing Technological Solutions to Non-participation in Adult Learning' *British Educational Research Journal* Vol. 26, No. 4, pp. 507–521

Green, Pat and Webb, Sue (1997) 'Student Voices: Alternative Routes, Alternative Identities.' in Williams, Jenny (ed) *Negotiating Access to Higher Education* Buckingham: SRHE/ Open University Press

Greenaway, David and Haynes, Michelle (2000) *Funding Universities to meet National and International Challenges* Nottingham: University of Nottingham. http://www.nottingham.ac.uk/economics/funding

Grenfell, Michael and James, David (1998) *Bourdieu and Education* London: Falmer

Harding, Sandra (1987) *Feminism and Methodology* Milton Keynes: Open University Press

Hardy, Thomas (1969) *Jude the Obscure* London: Macmillan

Haselgrove, Susanne (ed) (1994) *The Student Experience* Buckingham: SRHE/Open University Press

Higher Education Funding Council of England (HEFCE), (2000) *University Performance Indicators* www.educationunlimited.co.uk

Higher Education Funding Council of England (2001) *Partnerships for Progression: Proposals by the HEFCE and the Learning and Skills Council* Bristol: HEFCE

hooks, bell (1984) *Feminist Theory: from margin to centre* Boston: South End Press

Hugman, Richard and Smith, David (1995) *Ethical Issues in Social Work* London: Routledge

Huston, Anne Marshall (1992) *Understanding Dyslexia* London: Madison Books

James, David (1995) 'Mature Studentship in Higher Education: beyond a species approach' *British Journal of Sociology* Vol.16, No. 4, pp. 451–466

James, David (1998) 'Higher Education Field-work: The Interdependence of Teaching, Research and Student Experience' in Grenfell, Michael and James, David *Bourdieu and Education* London: Falmer

Jary, David and Parker, Martin (1998) *The New Higher Education: Issues and Directions for the Post-Dearing University* Stoke on Trent: Staffordshire University Press

Kemmis, Stephen and Wilkinson, Mervyn (1998) 'Participatory Action Research and the Study of Practice' in Atweh, Bill, Kemmis Stephen and Weeks, Patricia *Action Research in Practice: Partnerships for Social Justice in Education* London: Routledge

Knowles, John (2000) 'Access for the Few? Student Funding and its impact on Aspirations to Enter Higher Education.' *Widening Participation and Lifelong Learning* Vol. 2, No. 1, pp. 14–23

Larsen, Nella (1986) *Quicksand and Passing* New Brunswick N.J.: Rutgers University Press

Lather, Patti (1991) Getting Smart: Feminist Research and Pedagogy with/in the Postmodern London: Routledge

Lather, Patti and Smithers, Chris (1997) *Troubling the Angels: Women living with HIV and AIDS* Oxford: Westview Press

Lave, Jean and Wenger, Etienne (1991) *Situated Learning: Legitimate peripheral participation* Cambridge: Cambridge University Press

Leonard, Madeleine (1994) 'Transforming the Household: Mature Women Students and Access to Higher Education.' in Davies, Sue, Lubelska, Cathy and Quinn, Jocey (eds) *Changing the Subject: Women in Higher Education* London: Taylor and Francis

Livingstone, David, W. (1987) *Critical Pedagogy and Cultural Power* London: Macmillan

Lucase, Lisa and Webster, Frank (1998) 'Maintaining Standards in Higher Education? A Case Study' in Jary, David and Parker, Martin *The New Higher Education: Issues and directions for the post-Dearing University* Stoke on Trent: Staffordshire University Press

Lunneborg, Patricia (1994) *OU Women: Undoing Educational Obstacles* London: Cassell

Lynch, Kathleen (1989) *The Hidden Curriculum: Reproduction in Education, a Reappraisal* London: Falmer Press

Lynch, Kathleen (1999) *Equality in Education* Dublin: Gill and Macmillan

Mac an Ghaill, Mairtin (1989) 'Beyond the White Norm: The Use of Qualitative Methods in the Study of Black Youths' Schooling in England' *International Journal of Qualitative Studies in Education* Vol. 2, No. 3, pp. 175–89

Mahony, Pat (ed) (1997) *Class Matters: Working Class Women's Perspectives on Social Class* London: Taylor and Francis

McDonough, Patricia (1995) 'Structuring College Opportunities: A Cross-Case Analysis of Organizational Cultures, Climates and Habiti' in Torres, Carlos Alberto and Mitchell, Theodore, R. *Sociology of Education: Emerging Perspectives* Albany: State University of New York

McGivney, Veronica (1990) *Education's for Other People: Access to Education for Non-Participants* Leicester: NIACE

McGivney, Veronica (1996) *Staying on or Leaving the Course: Non-Completion and Retention of Mature Students in Further and Higher Education* Leicester: NIACE

McGivney, Veronica (1999) *Excluded Men: Men who are missing from education and training* Leicester: NIACE

McNair, Stephen (1997) 'Changing Frameworks and Qualifications' in Coffield, Frank and Williamson, Bill *Repositioning Higher Education* Buckingham: SRHE/Open University Press

Measor, Linda and Sikes, Patricia, (1992) *Gender and Schools* London: Cassell

Merrill, Barbara (1999) *Gender, Change and Identity* Aldershot: Ashgate

Moore, A. (1993) 'Genre, Ethnocentricity and Bilingualism in the English Classroom' in Woods, Peter and Hammersley, Martyn *Gender and Ethnicity in Schools: Ethnographic Accounts* London: Routledge

Moore, Rob and Muller, Johan (1999) 'The Discourse of "Voice" and the Problem of Knowledge and Identity in the Sociology of Education' *British Journal of Sociology of Education* Vol. 20, No. 2, pp. 189–206

Morrow, Raymond, and Torres, Carlos Alberto (1998) 'Social Closure, Professional Domination and the New Middle Strata: Rethinking Credentialist Theories of Education' in Torres, Carlos Alberto and Mitchell, Theodore *Sociology of Education: Emerging Perspectives* Albany: State University of New York

Oakley, Ann (1981) 'Interviewing Women: A Contradiction in Terms' in Roberts, Helen: *Doing Feminist Research* London: Routledge and Kegan Paul

Office for National Statistics (2000) *Social Trends* London: The Stationery Office

Olweus, Dan (1993) *Bullying at School: what we know and what we can do* Oxford: Blackwell

Open University (1999) *Widening participation and ethnic minority groups* Report EOC/9/8: Open University Equal Opportunities Committee: Milton Keynes: Open University

Open University (2000) *Student Registrations and Completion Rates 1997/8* Unpublished

Parr, Janet (2000) *Identity and Education: The Links for Mature Students* Aldershot: Ashgate

Pascall, Gillian and Cox, Roger (1993) *Women Returning to Higher Education* London: SRHE/Open University Press

Plummer, Gillian (2000) *Failing Working Class Girls* Stoke on Trent: Trentham Books

Preece, Julia (1999) *Combating Social Exclusion in University Adult Education* Aldershot: Ashgate

Purcell, Kate 'Ageism and Diversity in Recruitment' Speech to CVCP Conference: *Mature Students: encouraging participation and achievement* October 10th 2000

Reay, Diane (1995) ' "They Employ Cleaners to Do That": Habitus in the primary classroom' *British Journal of Sociology of Education* Vol. 16, No. 3, pp. 353–371

Reay, Diane (1998) *Class Work: Mothers' Involvement in Their Children's Primary Schooling* London: UCL Press

Rigby, Ken (1997) *Bullying in Schools* London: Jessica Kingsley

Robbins, Derek (1993) 'The Practical Importance of Bourdieu's Analysis of Higher Education' *Studies in Higher Education* Vol. 18, No. 2, pp. 151–163

Roberts, Helen (ed) (1981) *Doing Feminist Research* London: Routledge and Kegan Paul

Sanders, Clare (2000) 'Is Social work Becoming and Outcast' *Times Higher Education Supplement* 21st April 2000

Sharpe, Sue (1976) *Just Like a Girl: How Girls Learn to be Women* Harmondsworth: Penguin

Simons, Helen (ed) (1980) *Towards a Science of the Singular* University of East Anglia: Centre for Applied Research in Education

Smithers, Alan and Griffin, Alice (1986) *The Progress of Mature Students* Manchester: Joint Matriculation Board

Spender, Dale (1982) *Just Like a Woman: The Schooling Scandal* London: Writers and Readers Publishing Co-operative Society

Stake, Robert E. (1995) *The Art of Case Study Research* London: Sage

Swann, Lord (1985) *Education for All: A brief guide* London: HMSO

Tattum, Delwyn (1993) *Understanding and Managing Bullying* Oxford: Heinemann

Tattum, Delwyn and Herbert, Graham (1993) *Countering Bullying* Stoke on Trent: Trentham Books

Torres, Carlos Alberto and Mitchell, Theodore (eds) (1995) *Sociology of Education: Emerging Perspectives* Albany: State University of New York

Weil, Susan (1986) 'Non-traditional Learners Within Traditional Higher Education Institutions: Discovery and Disappointment' *Studies in Higher Education* Vol. 11, No. 3, pp. 219–235

Weil, Susan (1989) *Influences of Lifelong Learning on Adults' Expectations and Experiences of Returning to Formal Learning Contexts* PhD thesis: University of London: Institute of Education

Wenger, Etienne (1998) *Communities of Practice: Learning, Meaning and Identity* Cambridge: Cambridge University Press

Wickham, Ann (1986) *Women and Training* Milton Keynes: Open University Press

Willis, Paul (1977) *Learning to Labour: How Working Class Kids Get Working Class Jobs* Farnborough: Saxon House

Wolcott, H. (1994) *Transforming Qualitative Data* London: Sage

Woodley, Alan, Wagner, Leslie, Slowey, Maria, Hamilton, Mary and Fulton, Oliver (1987) *Choosing to Learn: Adults in Education* Oxford: Open University Press/SRHE

Woodrow, Maggie (1999) 'The Struggle for the Soul of Lifelong Learning' *Journal of Widening Participation and Lifelong Learning* Vol. 1, No. 1, pp. 9–12

Woods, Peter (1984) 'The Myth of Subject Choice' in Hammersley, Martyn and Woods, Peter (eds) (1984) *Life in School: The Sociology of Pupil Culture* Milton Keynes: Open University Press

Woods, Peter (1990) *The Happiest Days? How Pupils Cope with School* London: Falmer Press

Wright, Cecile (1993) 'School Processes: An ethnographic study' in Woods, Peter and Hammersley, Martyn *Gender and Ethnicity in School: ethnographic accounts* London: Routledge

Wright, Peter (1989) 'Putting the Learner at the Centre of Higher Education' in Fulton Oliver (ed) *Access and Institutional Change* Milton Keynes: SRHE/Open University Press

Young, Michael F.D. (ed) (1971) *Knowledge and Control: New Directions for the Sociology of Education* London: Collier Macmillan

INDEX